The World According to NARNIA

THE WORLD ACCORDING TO

NARNIA

Christian Meaning
in C. S. Lewis's Beloved
Chronicles

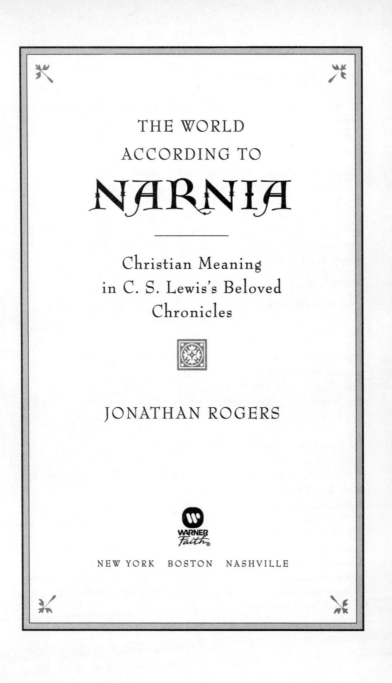

JONATHAN ROGERS

WARNER
Faith®

NEW YORK   BOSTON   NASHVILLE

Unless otherwise noted, Scriptures are taken from the New American Standard Bible®, Copyright © 1960, 1962, 1963, 1968, 1972, 1975, 1977, 1995 by The Lockman Foundation. All rights reserved.

Scriptures noted KJV are taken from the King James Version of the Bible.

Scriptures noted NIV are from the HOLY BIBLE, NEW INTERNATIONAL VERSION®. NIV®. Copyright © 1973, 1978, 1984 by International Bible Society. Used by permission of Zondervan. All rights reserved.

Warner Faith

Time Warner Book Group
1271 Avenue of the Americas, New York, NY 10020
Visit our website at www.twbookmark.com

The Warner Faith name and logo are registered trademarks of the Time Warner Book Group.
Printed in the United States of America
First Warner Faith printing: November 2005
10   9   8   7   6   5   4   3   2

Library of Congress Cataloging-in-Publication Data
Rogers, Jonathan.
    The world according to Narnia : Christian meaning in C.S. Lewis's beloved chronicles / Jonathan Rogers.
        p. cm.
    "Warner faith."
    ISBN 0-446-69649-8
1. Lewis, C. S. (Clive Staples), 1898-1963. Chronicles of Narnia. 2. Christianity and literature—England—History—20th century. 3. Children's stories, English—History and criticism. 4. Christian fiction, English—History and criticism. 5. Fantasy fiction, English—History and criticism. 6. Narnia (Imaginary place) I. Title.
    PR6023.E926C5367 2005
    823'.912—dc22   2005015960

For Lou Alice, near and far.

CONTENTS

Contents

ACKNOWLEDGMENTS

Steve Wilburn's fingerprints are all over this book, from the title on. His rigorous standards spurred me to write a better book than I could have written without him. I'm also thankful to John Eames, whose vigilance opened the first of many doors for *The World According to Narnia*. Thank you, Gary Terashita, for shepherding this book to completion. Particular thanks go to my wife and family who, as always, made many sacrifices during the last push toward the deadline for this book. And some credit must surely go to my parents and sisters, who taught me how to read and write and have been a source of much encouragement ever since.

Imagining Reality

 C. S. Lewis once received a letter from the mother of a nine-year-old boy named Laurence. Laurence was afraid the Chronicles of Narnia had led him into idolatry: he felt he loved the Great Lion Aslan more than he loved Jesus. What, the mother wanted to know, should she say to her son?

Lewis always took the sensitivities of children seriously, and his response to the boy's concerns was characteristically thoughtful and reassuring. He wrote: "Laurence can't *really* love Aslan more than Jesus, even if he feels that's what he's doing. For the things he loves Aslan for doing or saying are simply the things Jesus really did and said. So that when Laurence thinks he is loving

Aslan, he is really loving Jesus: and perhaps more than he ever did before."[1]

That, really, is how the Narnia stories do their work on you. Instead of giving you a lecture on the importance of staying warm, Lewis builds a fire and says, "Here—feel this." You can hardly help but love Aslan for the things he says and does. You can hardly help but desire what's good and right and true. You can hardly help but feel that a life of virtue is an adventure you wouldn't want to miss.

Christianity begins with a set of facts to believe, presented in the form of a story: God became a man, lived a perfect life, died to pay for the sins of his people, and rose again to lead them into heaven. But faith, in the end, isn't just about acknowledging truths, even truths as important as those. The demons believe that set of facts. The facts can matter to us—really matter—only if they are translated to our wills and desires. And that happens by way of the imagination. As Lewis put it, "Reason is the natural order of truth; but imagination is the organ of meaning."[2]

Elsewhere he makes the point that if it weren't for the imagination, the immensity of the universe would be no more awe-inspiring than the proliferation of numbers in the telephone directory: "Men look on the starry heavens with reverence: monkeys do not."[3] Imagination is a serious business. It gives substance to our yearnings for something beyond ourselves. Imagination is what convinces us that there's more to the world than meets the eye. And isn't that the first principle of faith?

As young Laurence found, the truths of the gospel can leave a believer cold. That's not a comment on the gospel or its power, but rather a comment on the state of the human heart, which can sleep through whole hurricanes of love and grace. The gospel permeates the life of the believer by way of the imagination. The Chronicles of Narnia awaken the reader to the imaginative possibilities of the gospel that have been there all along. The Chronicles serve as a reminder that if the gospel doesn't fill you with overwhelming awe and joy and fear and hope, you may not have really understood what the gospel says.

.✦.

One of the delicious ironies of Narnia is the fact that Lewis so carefully constructs a world of metaphor in order to insist that the God of the Bible is not a mere metaphor. Throughout the Chronicles, characters who think they're using imaginative language turn out to be talking about real life. Digory's Aunt Letty idly wishes for "fruit from the land of youth" to heal Digory's mother; Digory goes to the land of youth and fetches some. In *Prince Caspian*, Trumpkin the dwarf thinks Susan's horn of help is make-believe, but once he hears it, he wonders why nobody blew it sooner. In *The Silver Chair*, Jill Pole sees a peculiar line of huge rocks and wonders if they might have given rise to legends of giants in the North. Then the rocks stand up and reveal themselves to be real giants!

Lewis can be unsparing toward those who would reduce Aslan to an abstraction or an idea rather than a living, breathing lion, more real than the whole world put together. Consider the scene toward the end of *The Horse and His Boy* in which Bree, a rather self-satisfied talking horse, tries to explain his concept of Aslan to Hwin and Aravis:

> "No doubt," continued Bree, "when they speak of him as a Lion, they only mean he's as strong as a lion or (to our enemies, of course) as fierce as a lion. Or something of that kind. Even a little girl like you, Aravis, must see that it would be quite absurd to suppose he is a real lion. Indeed it would be disrespectful. If he was a lion he'd have to be a beast just like the rest of us. Why!" (and here Bree began to laugh) "If he was a lion he'd have four paws, and a tail, and *Whiskers!* "

Enamored of his own voice, his eyes half-closed with smug superiority, Bree doesn't notice what Hwin and Aravis can't miss: that Aslan the Great Lion is approaching from behind.

The brush of Aslan's whisker against his ear is enough to send Bree running for terror and for shame at having been such a fool. Aslan appears on the scene with an alarming reality that makes the "real world" seem pale and shadowy by comparison. "Touch me," Aslan insists. "Here are my paws, here is my tail, these are my whiskers." Aslan is no abstraction but a true beast, as concrete as Bree himself. It is a supremely Narnian moment: the old, familiar story of Doubting Thomas springs vividly to life as the reader comes to terms with what it would be like to be face-to-face with God made flesh.

In the end, things work out well for Bree because he realizes he is a fool and he wishes to be wise. Uncle Andrew, the magician of *The Magician's Nephew*, doesn't fare so well. As Lewis writes, "What you see and hear depends a good deal on where you are standing; it also depends on what sort of person you are." And Uncle Andrew is the kind of person who can't see any reality beyond the one he has created for himself.

Uncle Andrew, like Digory, Polly, and Frank the cabman, is on hand at the creation of Narnia. But whereas the others are enraptured by Aslan's creation song and the miracle of a world appearing where no world had been before, Andrew is so self-absorbed and terrified that he misses the whole thing.

When the Lion had first begun singing, long ago when it was still quite dark, he had realized that the noise was a song. And he had disliked the song very much. It made him think and feel things he did not want to think or feel. Then, when the sun rose and he saw that the singer was a lion ("*only* a lion," as he said to himself) he tried his hardest to make believe that it wasn't singing and never had been singing—only roaring as a lion in a zoo in our own world. "Of course it can't really have been singing," he thought, "I must have imagined it."

It takes imagination to step outside one's presuppositions. Andrew's materialist worldview doesn't allow for talking animals. In the absence of imagination, Andrew finds it easier to explain away the things he sees and hears than to come to terms with them. He understands growling and barking. He understands fear. But he's lost the ability to understand a miracle when he sees one. "The trouble about trying to make yourself stupider than you really are," writes Lewis, "is that you very often succeed."

Over and over again, the Narnia books demonstrate that imagination is more than just make-believe. Sometimes it takes imagination to see what's right in front of your face. It's the way we step outside ourselves, challenge our assumptions. *Imagination*, you might say, is just another word for *open-mindedness*.

But we must not make the mistake of thinking that Narnia represents the triumph of imagination over reason. Rather, it represents the triumph of reason and good sense by way of imagination. Consider Peter and Susan's conversation with Professor Kirke in chapter 5 of *The Lion, the Witch and the Wardrobe*. Lucy's insistence that she has been to Narnia has made them suspect she's going mad—especially since she claims to have been there with Edmund, who denies the whole thing. But when they express their concern to the professor, his response astonishes them: "'How do you know,' he asked, 'that your sister's story is not true?'"

It's a moment of real enlightenment for Peter and Susan. They had been unable to reason out the contradictions between Lucy's story and Edmund's because they were starting from the wrong set of presuppositions. As the professor makes clear, to say that a thing is unexpected or even unprecedented is not, logically speaking, the same thing as saying it's impossible or untrue.

The professor doesn't defy reason. Rather, he insists on a more rigorous logic than Peter and Susan had applied before. There are three logical possibilities, according to the professor: Lucy is lying, Lucy is insane, or Lucy is telling the truth. From a strictly logical point of view, the third possibility—that Lucy is telling the truth—seems at least as likely as the other two. And yet pure logic doesn't seem to be enough to justify such an unexpected conclusion. It takes a certain amount of imagination even to leave such a possibility on the table.

That's what Narnia means: shedding your preconceived notions of what's true and real and opening yourself up to the possibility that your categories—or the categories that have been foisted upon you—aren't sufficient to make sense of the world in which you live. Lewis uses fantasy to talk about the real world because it takes imagination to see what's true and real in this world too. The very basis of the Christian life is the ability to stand outside this world and see that this isn't all there is. From where we sit, the things of earth look so real and solid that it's hard to believe there's something more real and more solid; it's hard even to leave that possibility on the table. It takes a certain amount of imagination to see that God imbues every blade of grass, every conversation, every relationship with eternal meaning. It takes imagination to feel the truth of the gospel in our truest selves.

Every fantasy story takes its readers to another world. But Lewis never seems content to leave his readers there. With the exception of *The Last Battle*, the Friends of Narnia are jolted back to their own world at the end of each of the books. There they are required to carry on with the lives they had left behind. And so is the reader. At the end of *The Voyage of the Dawn Treader*, Edmund and Lucy are dismayed to learn that they won't be coming back to Narnia. They will stay on earth for the rest of their lives, but Aslan will be there, too, the Great Lion assures them: "But there I have another name. You must learn to know me by that name. This was the very reason why you were brought to Narnia, that by knowing me here for a little, you may know me better there."

The same is true for you. As you make your own journeys through Narnia, may you know the Lion better here.

The World According to NARNIA

CHAPTER ONE

Reality You Could Not Have Guessed
The Lion, the Witch and the Wardrobe

 "Reality," wrote C. S. Lewis, "is usually something you could not have guessed. That is one of the reasons I believe Christianity. It is a religion you could not have guessed."[1] When Lucy comes back out of the wardrobe after her first couple of visits to Narnia, Peter and Susan disbelieve her story because it's not something they would have guessed. For Professor Kirke, the very unlikelihood of her story is one of the reasons he believes it. If she were making it up, wouldn't she have made up something more plausible? If she were going to pretend to have been in another world for several hours, wouldn't she have hidden in the wardrobe for more than a minute? Surely no one so young could have invented the idea of a world where time runs differently from time on earth.

"But do you really mean, Sir," asks Peter, "that there could be other worlds—all over the place, just round the corner—like that?"

"Nothing is more probable," answers the professor. He speaks for that other professor, Professor Lewis. Indeed, he speaks for all mere Christians. For the most fundamental tenet of the faith is that there *is* another world (if you can call it that) just around the corner. A chief concern of the Christian faith is how to get from this world to that one. And the means by which we get from here to there are not what you would have guessed.

In the Chronicles of Narnia, we see a fictional outworking of a thought experiment from the second chapter of Lewis's book *Miracles*. What if, outside the vast system we call Nature (we might also call it the Universe) there existed other Natures? Each of these Natures would be as self-contained as ours; parts would be interlocked in space-time relationships and causal relationships, but they would have no such relationships with any part of this universe. Which is to say, under normal circumstances, no amount of travel could get you to one of those other Natures, and no action within this Nature could produce a reaction in one of those Natures. "This does not mean that there would be absolutely no relation between [different Natures]," says Lewis; "they would be related by their common derivation from a single Supernatural source. They would, in this respect, be like different stories by a single author."[2] The true connection between any two Natures exists in the mind of the Maker, to borrow a phrase from Dorothy Sayers.

Now, if two such Natures ever did come into contact somehow, each would be supernatural to the other; Lucy is no less supernatural to Tumnus than Tumnus is to her. "But the fact of their contact would be supernatural in a more absolute sense," Lewis continues—"not as being beyond this or that Nature, but beyond any and every Nature."[3] Whether or not Lewis believed in the existence of other Natures, he did believe in the existence of a transcendent Supernature. To step through the wardrobe is not only to see Narnia, but to get a glimpse of the mind of the Maker, which exists beyond this and all other worlds, and out of which they all derive.

In *Peter Pan*, Neverland is the geography of the Darling children's inner world. When Mrs. Darling peeks into her children's minds, she finds maps of Neverland. Before Peter Pan climbs in the nursery window, he already exists in the Darlings' imaginations. Narnia and the Pevensie children's relationship to it are another matter altogether. The Pevensies may enjoy rich imaginative lives, but their imaginations do not give rise to Narnia any more than they give rise to London or Professor Kirke's house. They explore, they play hide-and-seek, they climb trees and swim and lie in the heather. But we never hear of them playing make-believe. Lewis is careful from the start not to leave the possibility that Narnia is a figment of anybody's imagination. As peculiar as it seems, the world on one side of the wardrobe is as real as the world on the other. "We take reality as it comes to us," Lewis writes: "there is no good jabbering about what it ought to be like or what we should have expected it to be like."[4]

As if to underscore Narnia's reality, Lewis lovingly renders Tumnus's cave as a place of snug hominess. Except for the fact that he's a faun, Tumnus might be an English householder. He sits Lucy down in front of a cozy fire and serves her just the sort of tea she might get at home. The stories he tells of Narnia—of nymphs and dryads and summer dances, of red dwarfs and treasure hunts, of the feasts of Bacchus and Silenus—are fantastic to be sure, but the familiar domesticity of his little cave is the overruling impression of Lucy's first visit.

It is Lucy, in fact, who seems the figure of myth in this scene. She is the supernatural being who is intruding on the everyday life of the faun. Tumnus was merely going about his business. And if Tumnus isn't what Lucy expected to find when she stepped through the wardrobe in the spare room, Lucy surely isn't what Tumnus was expecting to find while walking home with an armload of parcels. A book on Tumnus's shelf asks *Is Man a Myth?*

The answer sits in his living room drinking his tea. For Tumnus, Lucy is much more than a little girl who has blundered into his forest. She is the "Daughter of Eve from the land of Spare Oom where eternal summer reigns around the bright city of War Drobe." He doesn't have it quite right, of course, but he does understand that she is a central figure in the mythology of Narnia.

But for all the hominess of Tumnus's cave, Narnia is enemy-occupied territory. The usurping White Witch rules in Narnia, and hers is a tyrannical rule. She has made it always winter. She is the spirit of death settled over the land. Death-white herself, she has managed to stop the life-giving cycle of the seasons whereby life springs forth from winter's pall. She has managed even to take away Christmas, that one spark of life and joy in the middle of the year's dead time. By banishing joy from the realm, she hopes to cut down all signposts leading back to her great enemy, Aslan. The least sign of joy represents a weakening of her power. Misery is the White Witch's only happiness. It's the only sign that she is still in charge.

The overthrow of the White Witch begins in Tumnus's cave, when Tumnus tearfully admits that he is the witch's agent, a hired kidnapper. Tumnus is one of those rare figures who repents of his sins before he ever realizes he has the need. His act of common decency, refusing to harm a girl who has never done him any harm, is the story's first act of rebellion against the White Witch. He lets Lucy go in the full knowledge that he may be tortured or turned to stone. This act of self-sacrifice is a faint echo of Aslan's greater sacrifice, on which the whole story hinges. By a simple but very difficult act of love, Tumnus keeps alive the hope that two Sons of Adam and two Daughters of Eve will sit on the four thrones at Cair Paravel.

When Edmund comes through the wardrobe and discovers that Lucy's "imaginary country" isn't imaginary after all, he doesn't have the good fortune of finding a friendly Narnian. He finds—or is found by—the White Witch. The White Witch knows the old lore of Narnia as well as anyone does; she certainly knows what it means to have a Son of Adam in her dominion. "This may wreck all," she mutters to herself. But she is crafty, and she is determined not to lose her grip on Narnia.

At first, Edmund is so terrified of the witch that he can't even move. Even when the White Witch drops her menacing manner and invites him into her sled with mock solicitude, Edmund obeys her out of fear, not out of any hope of real warmth or comfort underneath her mantle.

But Edmund is a boy of appetites, and it is through his belly that the witch wins him to her side. The White Witch's rule over Narnia has been defined by the removal or destruction of whatever joys and pleasures she can remove or destroy. So when she offers Edmund the seemingly simple pleasure of a hot drink on a winter's day, it is with the intention of taking all other pleasures away from him. From the time he drinks the witch's potion and eats her Turkish Delight, Edmund loses every defense that might have protected him from her. Giving himself over to his animal appetites, he becomes something less than human.

Greed and gluttony overcome all the better tendencies in Edmund, including his table manners. But the witch, who was at first very stern when Edmund didn't treat her with the courtly manners due a queen, is no longer bothered by his egregious breaches of courtesy. She is greedy, too, and she loves power more than she loves her own dignity.

Soon Edmund is so busy shoveling Turkish Delight into his mouth that it doesn't occur to him to wonder why the witch should be so interested in his brothers and sisters. The more he eats, the more he wants to eat of the enchanted confection. The hook is set. A few minutes earlier, Edmund had been terrified at the thought of being carried off on the witch's sledge. Now he begs the White Witch to carry him to her house, in hopes of getting more Turkish Delight.

The White Witch's feigned kindness has shaded over

into outlandish flattery and false promises. In his single-minded greed for more Turkish Delight, Edmund has grown so foolish that the White Witch need not exercise any particular subtlety anymore. It doesn't strike Edmund as strange that she would consider this sticky, red-faced, swinishly greedy boy the "cleverest and most handsome young man I've ever met." It begins to make perfect sense to Edmund that this magnificent queen should want to adopt him as a prince and later make him king of Narnia. His sense of superiority seems to grow, in fact, the deeper he sinks into swinishness. When the White Witch asks to be introduced to Edmund's brothers and sisters in order to make them courtiers in Edmund's court, Edmund's answer is telling: "There's nothing special about *them*." What began as a simple sin of appetite quickly begins to express itself in other, more spiritual sins.

By the time he is reunited with Lucy, Edmund is already feeling a little sick from the Turkish Delight. When he hears from his sister that the queen is really a witch, he feels even more uncomfortable. It's worth noting that Edmund does not doubt that Lucy is telling the truth about the woman he calls "the queen." Later he will pretend to doubt, of course, and the witch, by warning him about the unreliability of fauns, has given him the raw material from which to build a lie. But there in the forest, with the first wave of nausea from the Turkish Delight coming on him,

Edmund knows the truth about his patron and benefactress. Nevertheless, "he still wanted to taste that Turkish Delight again more than he wanted anything else."

Back on this side of the wardrobe, it becomes apparent that Edmund is not just a glutton and a fool, but a traitor also. The narrator describes Edmund's betrayal of Lucy as "one of the nastiest things in the story." It certainly is. Lucy believes she will be vindicated at last. It never occurs to her that her brother might lie—or even have reason to lie—about their adventure. But Edmund's generalized bad temper has crystallized into premeditated spite. When he denies having been to Narnia, he breaks Lucy's heart. Like his mistress, the White Witch, Edmund takes pleasure in taking good and innocent pleasures away from others. The witch's hold on him reaches across worlds all the way to England.

When all four Pevensies make it into Narnia at last, Edmund is exposed for a liar and a traitor. It's one of many chances he has to admit his guilt and be restored to his brother and sisters. Instead, he convinces himself that he is more sinned against than sinning. "I'll pay you all out for this, you pack of stuck-up, self-satisfied prigs," he mutters—as if the others had wronged him and not the other way around.

In spite of the cold, in spite of the fact that they have no food, the Pevensies decide to stay in Narnia in hopes of helping Tumnus. Lucy feels responsible for the faun's troubles with the White Witch. The children do not realize that it was Edmund, not Lucy, who betrayed Tumnus to the witch. And yet it is Edmund who votes against trying to help: "A lot *we* could do," he says, "when we haven't got anything to eat!" Edmund's appetite is still keeping him from doing the right thing.

Not knowing how else to start, the children follow a robin who seems to understand human speech and seems eager to help. Robins, as Peter points out, are always good birds in the stories he has read. This is the first instance of a theme that recurs throughout the Chronicles: the children know what to do because they have read the right imaginative stories.

Edmund isn't so sure the robin means them well—or at least he claims not to be sure. He frames his reluctance as a philosophical question: how do we know what we know? The faun said the queen was bad (Edmund still insists on calling her a "queen" rather than a "witch"). But who is to say the fauns are on the right side? It's not necessarily a bad question to ask. But coming from a boy who has met the White Witch, who has experienced her wickedness firsthand, the question is mere sophistry. It is his desire for Turkish Delight, not his desire for truth or caution, that motivates Edmund. Having raised the doubt in his brother's and sisters' minds, he doesn't seek out any resolution. Instead, he immediately changes the subject from doubt to fear: "Has anyone the least idea of the way home from here?" and from fear, Edmund moves immediately to his new favorite topic, his stomach. "And no chance of dinner either." He may talk of philosophical dilemmas, but in the end, this is all about Edmund's appetite.

✴

The Beavers' house is another sanctuary of warm domesticity in the icy world that is Narnia under the White Witch. Here the old ways of honor and hospitality and simple pleasures survive in spite of the witch's efforts. Mr. Beaver is the first person to utter the name *Aslan*. In the hopeful, conspiratorial tones of a resistance fighter, he whispers, "They say Aslan is on the move—perhaps has already landed." Though none of the Pevensies know who Aslan is, they know this is a name of "enormous meaning." But it's not the same meaning for all of them. For Edmund, who has already sided with Aslan's enemies, the name evokes "mysterious horror." Edmund doesn't know it yet, but Aslan means the death of everything he has come to value. Neither does he know, however, that the death of his old self means freedom to a new life.

For the other three Pevensies, the name of Aslan sounds like life in its fullness, not death: "Peter felt suddenly brave and adventurous. Susan felt as if some delicious smell or some delightful strain of music had just floated by her. And Lucy got the feeling you have when you wake up in the morning and realize that it is the beginning of the holidays or the beginning of summer." Strength, beauty, gladness—the approaching Aslan brings abundant life to those who rejoice to see him coming.

The Narnians cannot deliver themselves from the White Witch. Their only hope is Aslan, and Aslan is on the move. Not surprisingly, it is Edmund who wonders if the White Witch can turn Aslan into stone. Mr. Beaver laughs at the naïveté of the question: "The White Witch won't be able to look Aslan in the face, much less turn him to stone." The conflict between Aslan and the White Witch isn't a dualistic conflict between "two equal and independent powers."[5] Aslan is the source and origin of all that there is. It is in Aslan that all things, including the White Witch, "live and move and have [their] being" (Acts 17:28 NIV). She may seem invincible from the Narnians' perspective, but she has no real hope of overpowering Aslan. Twisted and perverse as she is, everything she has twisted and perverted is something she owes to Aslan. Lewis's description of Satan's rebellion against God applies equally to the White Witch's rebellion against Aslan: "It is like the scent of a flower trying to destroy the flower."[6]

Susan is always cautious, and when she learns that

Aslan is a lion, she is understandably hesitant. "Is he—quite safe? I shall feel rather nervous about meeting a lion." Aslan, of course, isn't safe, and anyone who doesn't experience fear in his presence is "either braver than most or else just silly." Aslan is not a tame lion, as Mr. Beaver says later in the story. But a tame lion isn't what the Narnians or the Pevensies want or need. Aslan isn't safe, but he's good. He invades Narnia with a terrifying, wild, and powerful goodness. He is somehow perfectly self-consistent and yet altogether unpredictable. Aslan's unpredictability—his ability to love in ways that nobody could have guessed—will soon save the rebellious Edmund and all of Narnia.

✴

In *Miracles* Lewis writes, "The slaves of the senses, after the first bait, are starved by their masters."[7] This truth is obvious enough to Edmund after he has trekked all the way to the White Witch's house and gotten only bread and water for his troubles. But he begins starving well before he gets to the witch's house. The memory of the Turkish Delight makes it impossible for him to enjoy the solid pleasures of the Beavers' meal. He can't enjoy the conversation either, convinced as he is that the others are snubbing him. The truth is, he can't enjoy anything anymore. He's an addict; he can think of nothing but his next fix of

Turkish Delight. As the demon Screwtape says, "An ever increasing craving for an ever diminishing pleasure is the formula."[8]

One of the surprising things about Edmund's journey is how much hardship he is willing to endure in order to damn himself. Virtue may be hard, but in this case it takes a perverse kind of self-discipline for Edmund to stay on the path of destruction. In the middle of a snowstorm, without a coat, he presses on instead of going back to the warmth and safety of the Beavers' house. He keeps himself going by mind games mostly. He imagines the improvements he will make to Narnia's infrastructure when he becomes king. He tells himself, in spite of his better judgment, that the witch has been good to him and is probably the rightful queen of Narnia anyway. He warms himself by stoking a growing hatred of Peter.

Arriving at the White Witch's house, Edmund feels the terror of the place. But he keeps going, telling himself it's too late to turn back now. His redoubled terror at the sight of the lion in the witch's courtyard is Edmund's last restraining impulse before he hands himself over to ruin. The stone lion reminds Edmund of whom he is really sinning against when he throws in his lot with the White Witch. But he doesn't avail himself of this last chance to turn back. When Edmund realizes that the lion is stone rather than flesh, he mistakes his relief for bravery. He bucks up his courage by telling himself that the statue is probably Aslan himself, defeated by the White Witch and her petrifying wand. "Pooh!" he says. "Who's afraid of Aslan?" What began as simple gluttony has now become blasphemy. Edmund pencils in a mustache and spectacles on the stone lion and jeers in its face: "Yah! Silly old Aslan! How do you like being a stone? You thought yourself mighty fine, didn't you?" And with that, Edmund steps the rest of the way into the White Witch's trap.

As that expert tempter Screwtape tells his nephew Wormwood, "The creatures are always accusing one another of wanting 'to eat the cake and have it'; but thanks to our labors, they are more often in the predicament of paying for the cake and not eating it."[9] Edmund has paid dearly for another bite of Turkish Delight. He has paid with his soul. But he won't be getting any more Turkish Delight from the White Witch. She is in the business of destroying pleasures, not handing them out. Now that she has Edmund in her clutches, she withholds even her false kindnesses and her empty promises. She wouldn't even give Edmund so much as bread and water if she didn't need to keep him alive a little while longer.

✳

Edmund may be in a trap, but Aslan is on the move. Kept out of Narnia for a hundred years, Father Christmas comes again to spread the merriment that the White Witch had banished. The witch manages to end the "gluttony, waste, and self-indulgence" of one Christmas party, but it is clear that she is fighting a losing battle. Her grip on Narnia is slipping. The winter, too, is losing its grip. New spring life is bursting out all over. The silence of the snowbound countryside gives way to the splash and bubble of moving water and the happy chirp of birdsong. The pallor of winter dissolves into the verdure and brightness of spring. "This is no thaw," says the witch's dwarf. "This is Spring . . . this is Aslan's doing."

✦

"People who have never been in Narnia sometimes think that a thing cannot be good and terrible at the same time." It is a hard idea to get one's mind around. But throughout the Chronicles of Narnia, when people come face-to-face with Aslan for the first time, they typically feel simultaneous joy and fear. It is worth noting that until recently *awesome* and *awful* meant the same thing. The old hymn says, "How sweet and awful is the place / With Christ within the doors." In the King James Version, the psalmist offers up praise that seems jarring to modern ears: "How terrible art thou in thy works!" (66:3). Solomon meant it when he said "The fear of the LORD is the beginning of knowledge" (Prov. 1:7).

When the Pevensies and the Beavers first see Aslan, they don't know what to do or say. The very sight of him is overwhelming. At last Peter steps forward to offer his services to the One who surely needs no help. The Pevensies have come to play their part in a drama they do not yet understand. But one of them is missing. It will take two Sons of Adam and two Daughters of Eve to fill the four thrones at Cair Paravel and end the reign of the White Witch. Edmund's treachery has jeopardized the future happiness of all Narnia. In Aslan Lucy sees One who can help what seems an impossible situation. "Please, Aslan," she asks, "can anything be done to save Edmund?" "All shall be done," Aslan answers. "But it may be harder than you think." Alongside the strength and peace on the Great Lion's face, Lucy thinks she sees a flash of sadness.

Edmund's physical rescue from the White Witch is achieved easily enough. But the White Witch has a claim on Edmund that is much stronger than the ropes by which she had bound him. Edmund is a traitor. And the Deep Magic—the very magic that holds Narnia together—requires that every traitor be handed over to the White Witch. She is, as Mr. Beaver puts it, "the Emperor's hangman." The Deep Magic is the Moral Law. It goes deeper than the statutes and legislation of a creaturely code of law, though all good laws derive from it. Its inexorable penalties do not ultimately depend on any creature for their enforcement. "There is nothing indulgent about the law," Lewis argues in *Mere Christianity*. "It is hard as nails. It tells you to do the straight thing, and it does not seem to care how painful, or dangerous, or difficult it is to do."[10] The Deep Magic is a good thing, established by Aslan's father, the Emperor, not by the witch. She is working the system, so to speak, to her own advantage, but it is not her system any more than Narnia is her country.

The White Witch has Edmund dead to rights, and it appears there is little Aslan can do about it. Though Aslan has strength enough to enforce his will on the White Witch, he cannot work against the Deep Magic. He cannot deny the truth of the White Witch's claim: "Unless I have blood as the Law says, all Narnia will be overturned and perish in fire and water." The laws are Aslan's laws and his father's. He has bound himself to them.

✦

Aslan has a plan to snatch victory out of what appears to be certain defeat. And it is not what anyone—least of all the White Witch—would have guessed. Without blood there is no remission of sins. The White Witch is entitled to blood for Edmund's crimes, and blood she will have. She will have Aslan's. The Deep Magic will be fulfilled.

When Aslan first strides up to the Stone Table where the sacrifice is to be made, the White Witch and all her horrible mob of followers are struck with fear. This is still Aslan, after all, and he can spring upon his enemies and destroy them all anytime he wants. But he doesn't. He submits himself to their jeering abuse. The White Witch, no doubt, is amazed at the success of her plan. She had hoped only to prevent the four thrones at Cair Paravel from being filled. Now she will see her invincible enemy dead. She can kill the Sons of Adam and Daughters of Eve at her leisure.

"The fool has come," the witch crows. In his generosity, in his eagerness to save Edmund, the Lion appears to have made a grave strategic error. This sort of self-sacrifice must appear to be the very height of foolishness to those who know nothing of love. "The word of the cross is foolishness to those who are perishing" (1 Cor. 1:18). It never occurs to the witch that she is the one who has walked into a trap.

The hags who bind Aslan shriek with triumph (and relief) when the Great Lion makes no resistance. The more the Great Lion submits, the more his enemies convince themselves that they have somehow defeated him. This is the same Lion who terrifies even his friends. A single roar would lay the whole mob flat. Yet, "like a lamb that is led to slaughter, / And like a sheep that is silent before its shearers, / So He did not open his mouth" (Isa. 53:7). It is not the cords that keep Aslan on the Stone Table. It is not the muzzle that keeps him from swallowing his enemies whole. It is his terrible love. His humiliations are all part of the plan. And the witch's mob still hasn't guessed it. Before she kills the Lion, the witch cannot help gloating: "And now who has won?" That question will be answered soon enough.

As Lewis argues in *Miracles*, one combatant's master-stroke may be "the very means by which the superior combatant defeats him. Every good general, every good chess-player, takes what is precisely the strong point of his opponent's plan and makes it the pivot of his own plan."[11] Death is the White Witch's weapon of choice. Surely the death of Aslan would mean irreversible victory. But after Aslan's death, the pivot turns and the White Witch's plan comes thundering down around her.

The Stone Table cracks. The Deep Magic from the Dawn of Time has been fulfilled. It has been superseded by a Deeper Magic. The White Witch could see back only as far as Narnia's creation. But before that, when there were only stillness and darkness, there was the Deeper Magic from which the Deep Magic—the Moral Law—grew. Within that Deeper Magic is another incantation, one the witch had no way of knowing: "When a willing victim who had committed no treachery was killed in a traitor's stead, the Table would crack and Death itself would start working backwards." Aslan has come to bring new life to Narnia. He has come bearing springtime. Now death will be overturned in earnest.

When Edmund ran afoul of the Deep Magic, he let himself into a vicious circle from which he had no way of escape. Lewis summarizes the dilemma that every sinner, Edmund included, faces: "Only a bad person needs to repent: only a good person can repent perfectly." Putting it another way, he writes, "But the same badness which makes us need [repentance] makes us unable to do it. Can we do it if God helps us? Yes, but what do we mean when we talk of God helping us?"[12] The help Aslan offers to Edmund is to break into his vicious circle and serve as what Lewis called the "perfect penitent."[13]

For Edmund to die for his own sins is only to bring the balance back up to zero. When a perfect substitute—one with no sins of his own to die for—dies for the sins of another, it changes the whole economy. The Deeper Magic of love and self-sacrifice reverses the death that had been the wages of sin. " 'Tis mystery all." The death and resurrection of Aslan don't fully explain the Christian doctrine of the atonement, in large part because Lewis never claimed to understand the mechanics of the atonement himself. But it does give us a stirring picture of what it means that the atonement *does* work. The awe of coming face-to-face with the terrible beauty of Aslan gives way to the even deeper awe that such a being would subject himself to such humiliation for the sake of one who has openly rebelled against him. Even the angels long to look into such things.

Death works backward after Aslan's resurrection. Aslan opens Narnia not just to new life, but to abundant life of joy and honest pleasures. One of Aslan's first acts after coming back to life is a game of chase with Susan and Lucy; "and whether it was more like playing with a thunderstorm or playing with a kitten Lucy could never make up her mind." When Aslan invades the White Witch's house, the stone-cold whiteness of the place yields to the colors and textures and movement of Nature's bounty: "glossy chestnut sides of centaurs, indigo horns of unicorns, dazzling plumage of birds. . . . And instead of the deadly silence the whole place rang with the sound of happy roarings, brayings, yelpings, barkings, squealings, cooings, neighings, stampings, shouts, hurrahs, songs and laughter."

Aslan's happy army finishes off the enemy in short order, rescuing Peter and Edmund and their small band of fighters. Freed from the witch's clutches, Edmund fights as fiercely and as bravely as anyone. He is his own man again, his old self. He can look his brother and sisters in the face again.

The Pevensies take their place at Cair Paravel. They are the Kings and Queens of Narnia. This is their part in the drama of Narnia. This is what Aslan brought them here to do. But Aslan slips away. "He'll be coming and going," says Mr. Beaver. "It's quite all right. He'll often drop in. Only you mustn't press him. He's wild, you know. Not like a *tame* lion."

✦

"For My thoughts are not your thoughts,
Nor are your ways My ways," declares the LORD.
"For as the heavens are higher than the earth,
So are My ways higher than your ways,
And My thoughts higher than your thoughts." (Isaiah 55:8–9)

Or to say it another way, the real things are the things you would have never guessed. "Consider how we acquired the old, ordinary kind of life," says Lewis. That is to say, consider where babies come from. It is "a very curious process, involving pleasure, pain, and danger. A process you would have never guessed."[14] Is it any surprise, then, that the new life in Christ is acquired by a process you would have never guessed?

The God who is "terrible in his ways"—the God whose presence in a vision caused the prophet Isaiah to fall out in a dead swoon—is the same God who submitted himself to a humiliating death for the love of sinners like us. The Immortal died. The King of Heaven and Earth became poor for our sakes. The Lion of Judah sat as silent as a sheep before his shearers.

No, there's nothing predictable—or safe, for that matter—about the God of the Bible. But God is good. And in the end, omnipotence turns out to be the same thing as infinite love.[15] Who would have guessed it?

CHAPTER TWO

Myth Become Fact
Prince Caspian

 Four children sit in a sleepy little train station waiting for the trains that will take them back to school. What could be more mundane and unremarkable? And yet these four children are figures of myth in another world, the object of great longing and hope. On earth they are the Pevensie children. In Narnia, they are the Ancient Kings and Queens, the last hope of a heroic last stand by the Old Narnians.

Prince Caspian is a book about mythology and belief. At the center of the story is another story: the ancient legend of Queen Susan's horn. "Whoever blows it shall have strange help—no one can say how strange." From the reader's perspective, the help that comes is strange indeed. The story of *Prince Caspian* takes us all the way around the legend of Susan's horn, allowing us to investigate it from every side.

We experience what it's like to be Aladdin rubbing the lamp *and* what it's like to be the genie, summoned out of one world and into another. And surprisingly, the genie's ability to believe the story matters as much as Aladdin's. Actually, perhaps the most surprising thing may be that the belief of either one could shape a story that has another Author. It is belief that translates the power of the Old Stories into the affairs of humans and beasts.

To believe the Old Stories is to take part in them—to enact them in the world where we live. Prince Caspian learns that everything he ever hoped for turns out to be true after all. Yet this realization isn't an invitation to relax in its reassuring truth: it's a summons for Caspian to fight for what he believes. Belief and unbelief aren't just mental categories. Rather, they play themselves out in the world of action. Nikabrik's willingness to "believe in" anything or anyone who will help his side win the battle causes him to sell out his side to forces of evil much worse than the enemies the Old Narnians are fighting. Trumpkin's commitment to duty in spite of doubt finds its reward in true belief and triumph in battle. And even the Pevensies, the heroes of the story, find that belief is the only way to find their way.

✳

When they are drawn out of our world, the Pevensies find themselves in a fairy-tale world where everybody hasn't lived happily ever after, where the old mythologies appear to be irrelevant. There is little to recognize in the Narnia where Prince Caspian has spent his childhood. Caspian has never seen a talking animal or a dryad or even (so far as he knows) a dwarf. Narnia is an unhappy kingdom ruled by a cruel king. This isn't the first time we've seen Narnia under a wicked ruler. But even the White Witch's hundred-year winter was a distinctly Narnian kind of tyranny—a tyranny by enchantment. The tyranny of Miraz is much more prosaic, enforced not by magic, but by murder and high taxes and repressive laws. All sense of wonder—everything worth wondering at—seems to have fled.

This is the kingdom that Prince Caspian stands to inherit. But he longs for something more. His aunt and uncle, the king and queen, have sheltered him from the realities of Narnian life. They are raising him to be as banal as they are. They do not realize there is a spy of sorts in their household. Caspian's nurse tells him stories of the Old Days in Narnia, when animals could talk and naiads and dryads lived in the rivers and fauns lived in the forest. She tells him of High King Peter and King Edmund and Queens Susan and Lucy, and of Aslan's defeat of the White Witch. This is the Narnia that Caspian longs for. Even as a little boy, he feels the loss of separation from the Old Narnia that disappeared before he was born—if, indeed, it ever existed.

King Miraz dismisses such yearnings as foolishness.

Talking animals and dwarfs are baby talk, he insists, nursery stories not fit for a prince of Narnia. His apparent skepticism grows into open rage, however, at the mention of the name *Aslan*. "There's no such person as Aslan," he thunders. "And there are no such things as lions. And there was never a time when animals could talk."

The reader (assuming she has read *The Lion, the Witch and the Wardrobe* or any other of the Chronicles) knows full well that there is such a person as Aslan, and that, even if they don't talk now, there was a time when animals could talk in Narnia. The claim that there are no such things as lions seems especially preposterous. But little Caspian has no way of knowing what to believe. It's not clear what Miraz believes either—whether his vehemence arises from a desire to suppress a dangerous falsehood or a dangerous truth.

In any case, Miraz and his regime understand that the stories of Aslan and the Old Days represent a serious threat to their power. And since those stories won't go away, their best hope of suppressing them is to relegate them to the realm of the fairy tale—entertaining enough, but not something that any self-respecting adult would actually believe.

The fairy tale may or may not be the best repository for truth. It does, however, allow truth to hide in plain sight. As Caspian found, the nurse's fairy tales allowed the truth of Aslan to do its work on him quite as well as if it had been presented as history or even holy writ. Miraz and his ilk would dismiss the stories of Old Narnia as mere myth. But for Lewis, there was nothing "mere" about mythology. According to Lewis, myth at its best is "a real though unfocused gleam of divinity on the human imagination."[1] Myth speaks to those human yearnings for something beyond what the earth has to offer. Myth offers up truth as it is tasted and felt, not as it is reasoned out and memorized. It sits halfway between the abstraction of, say, philosophy and the concrete particularity of lived experience. So then, "in the enjoyment of a great myth, we come nearest to experiencing as a concrete what can otherwise be experienced only as an abstraction."[2] Good myths—even the ones that aren't literally true—are a window onto the reality that we cannot see.

Myths may speak truth, but they are not typically factual, in the way that historical records or multiplication tables are factual. Not *typically*. The incarnation of Christ is that unique instance in which myth became fact. "The heart of Christianity is a myth which is also a fact. The old myth of the Dying God, *without ceasing to be myth*, comes down from the heaven of legend and imagination to the earth of history. It *happens*—at a particular date, in a particular place, followed by definable historical consequences."[3] Plenty of myths awaken the heart's desire for heaven. One myth fulfills it.

Caspian is moving gradually toward the realization that

the myths he loves so much are fact. For now, they can only stir his longings, not fulfill them. But for now, the longing is enough. Whether or not the stories about Aslan turn out to be factual, to Caspian they feel truer than the facts of the world he sees around him. They speak to his imaginative self in a way that the dull world of court intrigues never will. The fairy tales have awakened in Caspian a longing that will draw him like a homing pigeon to his truest home, his truest self.

Fairyland, according to Lewis, arouses in a reader "a longing for he knows not what. It stirs and troubles him (to his lifelong enrichment) with the dim sense of something beyond his reach and, far from dulling or emptying the actual world, gives it new dimension and depth."[4] Caspian is one so troubled. Having been infected with a longing for the Old Narnia, he may never again be much use in the new Narnia of King Miraz—at least not in the way that the king would want him to be useful.

Miraz is understandably eager to separate Caspian from his nurse, but if his goal is to get his nephew's mind off Old Narnia, he could hardly have chosen a worse tutor than Dr. Cornelius. What Caspian's nurse offers up as fairy tale, Dr. Cornelius offers up as history. He confirms what Caspian has always hoped to be true: Narnia is Aslan's country. The silence of the trees and animals is not their natural state; they were silenced by the conquering Telmarines. For

Caspian, the sadness of the news is overcome by the joy of knowing that there once was a time when animals in Narnia could speak. "I *am* glad it was all true," he says, "even if it is all over."

That's a remarkable expression of the power of myth. Caspian doesn't hope for any tangible benefit from Aslan or the Old Narnians. All he gets is the satisfaction of knowing that his yearnings have not been empty. His longings have pointed toward something real. Caspian has all the tangible benefits of kingship to look forward to. And yet he sets his hopes on a world that, so far as he knows, is gone.

Caspian learns even more astonishing news: Dr. Cornelius is part dwarf himself. Old Narnia isn't so far off as Caspian had thought. His feelings on learning this are, on a smaller scale, the same contradictory feelings that characters throughout the Chronicles feel when they first encounter Aslan. First he fears for his life; he is the heir, after all, of the men who led the conquest of the happy people whom Dr. Cornelius represents. Caspian could hardly expect mercy, given the ruthlessness of the environment in which he grew up. But he also can't help feeling "pure delight" at knowing that dwarfs exist.

Caspian need not fear harm from Dr. Cornelius, however. If Dr. Cornelius represents hope to Caspian—hope that Old Narnia remains—Caspian represents a much greater hope to Dr Cornelius. For at least ten generations, the Telmarines have oppressed Old Narnia. Now at last a Telmarine who loves the Old Things is heir to the Narnian throne. Caspian is no longer just a devotee of the old stories. It is becoming apparent that he has a part to play in them himself.

Prince Caspian has moved, one step at a time, toward the realization that the myths of Aslan and Old Narnia are living facts. He goes from fairy tales to ancient history to recent history. Even so, coming face to face with Old Narnians—with a talking badger and two dwarfs—is much like stepping through the looking glass for Caspian. Believing in another world and actually going there are two very different things.

It has taken some time for Caspian to know what to believe about the Old Narnians. The Old Narnians, for their part, don't immediately know what to believe about Caspian either. Perhaps the most surprising thing about the Old Narnians is that they don't all believe the stories of Old Narnia themselves. Trufflehunter, the badger, comes from a race with long memories. He believes in Aslan without question and still lives by the old codes of honor and hospitality. But the dwarfs are considerably more pragmatic. Times have changed; and even if beasts don't change, dwarfs do. It has been many generations since belief in Aslan has offered any practical benefit. The dwarfs, therefore, don't believe.

Even so, it is apparent from the start that Trumpkin's disbelief is a different kind from Nikabrik's. Trumpkin is an honest dwarf, and his doubts are honest doubts. Nikabrik, on the other hand, is the worst sort of cynic; his disbelief is willful, of a piece with his bloody-minded and hateful view of the world. A lifetime of oppression has twisted his soul. The first words we hear from Nikabrik are a call to kill Caspian. He never really rises above that level.

One of the hallmarks of Nikabrik's mind is intellectual dishonesty. He trots out specious arguments in support of his prejudices and hatreds, but he won't be convinced by sound reasoning. He tries to turn Trufflehunter against Caspian by arguing that no one who has hunted beasts for sport could possibly be a friend to beasts. In his own defense, Caspian rightly points out that he has never hunted talking beasts. Nikabrik persists: "It's all the same thing." Trufflehunter, the voice of good faith and good sense, won't let him get away with it. The difference between talking beasts and dumb beasts is much greater than the difference between dwarfs and the half-dwarfs such as Dr. Cornelius, whom Nikabrik hates so passionately. You get the impression that this isn't the first time Trufflehunter has had to say, "No, Nikabrik, you know that's not true."

Nikabrik, like the rest of the black dwarfs, is at heart a politician, not a believer. Caspian is of interest to them only insofar as he can be useful in overthrowing the current regime. If he is an enemy of King Miraz, they will have him for a king. And if the Old Stories help galvanize the Old Narnians to fight the Telmarines, they are all for the Old Stories. But they are far too pragmatic and far too bitter for their hearts to be stirred by the thought of the rightful king coming into his own, or the thought of Aslan setting things right in Narnia.

The dwarfs are for the dwarfs, and they will gladly make alliances with anyone who will help them exact revenge on Miraz and his people. Their willingness to recruit Ogres and Hags to the cause doesn't bode well for the future. "I'll believe in anyone or anything," says Nikabrik, "that'll batter those cursed Telmarine barbarians to pieces or drive them out of Narnia. Anyone or anything, Aslan *or* the White Witch, do you understand?"

Prince Caspian, you'll remember, thrilled to hear the stories of Aslan and Old Narnia even when he believed they could do him no practical good. For Nikabrik and the black dwarfs, practicality is the only factor determining where they will place their trust. And in their case, practicality is defined in terms of what will empower them to act out their hatreds. The stories of Aslan and Old Narnia can't do their work on them. They cannot receive the blessings that the old stories promise. When the Old Narnians dance at Dancing Lawn—that is to say, when they go about the business of living the life for which they will soon be fighting—

Nikabrik can only look on from a distance. He's eager to fight, but it's not clear what he's fighting for.

Trumpkin is a much more agreeable fellow than Nikabrik. He is noble and fair-minded. He is a dwarf of conscience. He answers Nikabrik's abusive criticism with cool good sense. Nikabrik wants to kill Caspian for stumbling onto their hideout. Trumpkin points out that the boy didn't choose to bash his head against a tree at just that spot. Nikabrik wants to run Dr. Cornelius through for a renegade dwarf. Trumpkin points out that nobody chooses his ancestry. Trumpkin, in fact, talks and acts as a true Narnian should, except for the fact that he doesn't believe in Aslan or talking trees or, indeed, anything he hasn't seen with his own eyes. He exhibits the limitations of his people. But he is not without hope.

"A sane man," writes C. S. Lewis, "accepts or rejects any statement, not because he wants to or doesn't want to, but because the evidence seems to him good or bad."[5] Nikabrik may consider himself a realist, but he believes only what he wants to believe. All of his beliefs grow out of bitterness and hatred. They stand or fall quite independently of any assessment of the evidence. By contrast, Trumpkin's beliefs about Aslan, though false, are quite sane by Lewis's definition. He rejects the Old Stories because he isn't satisfied by the evidence.

The same evidence, by the way, has been adequate for Trufflehunter. Consider the difference between Trufflehunter and Trumpkin's reactions to Dr. Cornelius's counsel. The old half-dwarf advises that they retreat to long-forgotten Aslan's How in the eastern forest, where Telmarines have feared to go these many generations. "It is a good thing we have a learned man among us," says Trufflehunter, and he is eventually proven right. But Trumpkin's response is that of the pragmatist: "I wish our leaders would think less about these old wives' tales and more about victuals and arms."

Trumpkin, however, doesn't suppose his unbelief exempts him from doing his duty. Caspian has no subject more loyal than Trumpkin. When the Old Narnians decide that their only hope of victory lies with blowing Queen Susan's horn, Trumpkin doesn't believe it's a good idea. He has no hope of its helping, and he doesn't want to raise false hopes among the fighters. What's more, he doesn't like the idea of sending two badly needed fighters away from the theater of battle to rendezvous with the help for which he can't even bring himself to hope. And yet it is Trumpkin who makes the dangerous journey to meet Peter, Susan, Edmund, and Lucy. Nikabrik, not surprisingly, refuses: "With all these Humans and beasts about, there must be a Dwarf here to see that the Dwarfs are fairly treated." Nikabrik had voted for the blowing of the horn. But he doesn't believe in any way that might draw him out of his self-protective bitterness or cause him to leave off special-interest politics.

Trumpkin doesn't even pretend to hope. He only obeys. "I know the difference between giving advice and taking orders," he tells Caspian. "You've had my advice, and now it's the time for orders." Trumpkin's commitment to duty in the face of his disbelief will soon be rewarded with a belief that saves not only Trumpkin, but Narnia itself.

When Susan's horn blows, Trumpkin at last begins—but only just begins—to feel the truth of the Old Stories. When he describes the moment, it's the first time we hear the overly practical dwarf grow lyrical: "The whole air was full of it, loud as thunder but far longer, cool and sweet as music over water." And once he has heard the horn, he wonders why Caspian didn't blow it sooner. He's beginning to feel that ancient longing that afflicted Caspian. But belief is a process, for Trumpkin more so than for most believers. He has far to go before he surrenders himself to the truth that is just beginning to make itself unavoidable.

Trumpkin's rescue from his Telmarine captors is a moment of colliding mythologies. For generations, the Telmarines have haunted the forests near Cair Paravel with invented ghost stories—a false mythology to protect themselves from the true and (to them) dangerous mythology of Aslan. They have told the stories so long that they have begun to believe them. The truth imposes itself on the Telmarines' ghost stories with a force no less palpable than Susan's arrow ricocheting off the steel helmet of Trumpkin's captor. Yet, Trumpkin doesn't know how to make sense of what has happened. He has always heard these woods are full of ghosts; to his way of thinking, it seems as likely that he has been rescued by four ghosts as by the Ancient Kings and Queens.

Slowly it dawns on Trumpkin who these four children are. They are myth become fact. In Prince Caspian's case, you will remember, his imagination is captured by the mythology of Aslan long before the facts begin to reveal themselves. Trumpkin, however, suffers from a stunted imagination. Dwarfs are pragmatic folk, after all. He believes what he has seen, but *only as much as* he has seen. He believes the Pevensies are the four children out of the Old Stories, called into Narnia by way of Susan's horn. But he lacks the imagination to make the next, seemingly obvious step. Because the Ancient Kings and Queens are children, it never occurs to him that they could provide the help he has come looking for. After the children have demonstrated their warlike skills, Trumpkin at last believes that help has come, just as the Old Stories promised. But only because the facts are truly undeniable. He still hasn't exhibited faith.

What constitutes grounds for belief? It's a central question in *Prince Caspian*. For Caspian, his first glimpse of Old Narnians is proof positive that everything he had ever hoped about Aslan is true after all. The same humans who laugh at stories of Aslan laugh at stories of talking beasts and dwarfs too. So when Caspian sees dwarfs and talking beasts, any doubts he has had about Aslan melt away. It's not sound reasoning, of course, but Caspian's conviction has more to do with satisfied longing than satisfied reasoning. Genuine evidence will come soon enough.

Trumpkin and Nikabrik have spent every day of their lives in the world that so inspired Caspian, yet they no more believe in Aslan than King Miraz does. To Caspian they must seem like fish who do not believe in water. But then again, the disciples who walked with Jesus during his earthly ministry and witnessed his signs and wonders were more remarkable for their doubt than for their belief.

That being the case, perhaps it should not be surprising that the Pevensies experience their own struggles with belief. They are the heroes of the story, Narnia's salvation; they have seen Aslan face-to-face; they have come to Narnia by Aslan's intervention. To the Narnians, it would appear that the Ancient Kings and Queens should have no cause to doubt. But they do. They have been drawn into Narnia through no will of their own, but now that they are here, it will take an exercise of the will—an act of belief—

to finish their task. The paths through the woods are deceptive, and enemies are all around; they cannot find their way, cannot do their work without Aslan's guidance.

Lucy, as usual, is the first of the four to see the Great Lion. She is the least gifted in those skills that would seem to be most needed in a campaign to free Narnia from the Telmarines. She cannot shoot like Susan or fight like her brothers. But she can believe. Lucy's belief will prove to be the bridge by which the invading Aslan reenters Narnia.

Everyone but Lucy is sound asleep when she first feels the stirrings of Aslan's presence. Alone in the moon-dappled forest, she is pierced by a longing for the days when the trees could still talk in Narnia. She calls to the dryads and hamadryads to awaken, and she feels that they almost do. She can almost understand what the rustling trees are trying to say, but before she can put a finger on it, the woods go still again. Her experience recalls Lewis's own experience of that he calls "Joy," that "unsatisfied desire which is in itself more desirable than any other satisfaction."[6]

His first taste of this Joy came, oddly enough, from the sight of a toy garden his elder brother made by arranging moss and twigs and flowers in a biscuit tin. The beauty of it awakened in him a desire he couldn't put his finger on: "Before I knew what I desired, the desire itself was gone, the whole glimpse withdrawn, the world turned commonplace again, or only stirred by a longing for the longing that had just ceased."[7]

But if Lucy is stirred by a longing for the trees, the trees are stirred by their own longing for Lucy. "For the anxious longing of the creation waits eagerly for the revealing of the sons of God" (Rom. 8:19). It is not just the "people" of Narnia—the talking animals and dwarfs and fauns—who have been oppressed by the Telmarines. All the created order has been "subjected to futility," to use the words of the apostle Paul (Rom. 8:20). The redemption of Narnia will be a redemption of the whole natural world. And Lucy represents Narnia's best hope for redemption. She will soon be revealed in her truest self, and that revealing is what Narnia has been waiting and longing for.

When Lucy sees Aslan the next day, she is again the only one who is awake to the spiritual realities around her. No one else sees the Great Lion, who is leading up the gorge, against their natural inclinations. The group does the democratic, if not the obedient thing: they take a vote. They choose to walk by sight rather than faith. Instead of following the Lion they cannot see—and whose way is counterintuitive—they follow their own judgment, into great peril and hardship.

Edmund, it is worth noting, sides with Lucy. He learned his lesson the first time they came to Narnia; even though he lacks the sight to see Aslan for himself, he has sense enough to follow those who can. He shows a certain kinship with Trumpkin in this, knowing when to give his opinion and when to follow those who are in a position to lead. But Lucy and Edmund are overruled, and in letting themselves be overruled, they put themselves in a position to suffer the same hardships as the unbelievers.

When Lucy does come face-to-face with Aslan—again while everyone else is sleeping—she finds that the Great Lion has grown since she last saw him. In truth, it is Lucy's faith that has grown, not Aslan. He seems bigger because she can see more of him. But her faith still isn't big enough. Lucy has always been a follower. The youngest of the group and the least assertive, she hasn't shown the courage of her convictions. Aslan transforms Lucy's faith into the kind of faith that will transform Narnia. He starts by making Lucy take responsibility for her own decisions. Yes, the other members of the group have not believed, and they will be held accountable for their unbelief. But Aslan won't let Lucy blame anyone but herself for her choice to go with the group rather than follow his leading.

Lucy cannot see what *would* have happened had she followed Aslan up the gorge the first time. The Lion will show her many things, but not that. She closed the door on that future. A new future presents itself, a second chance, but it requires that Lucy submit to Aslan's plan. She had pictured

Aslan "roaring in" and routing the enemy as he had routed the army of the White Witch at Beruna. Aslan has another idea. Openness to Aslan's plans—whatever they might turn out to be—is a key component of faith. You might say such openness *is* faith. Aslan is not a tame lion, after all, and he can't be expected to stick too closely to anyone's preconceived notions of how he ought to do things.

In this case, Aslan requires that Lucy show the courage of a leader. He requires, in other words, that Lucy perform the role she seems least qualified to perform. He doesn't require that she do it in her own strength, however. Lucy buries her head in Aslan's mane, and in that gesture of weakness and fear, she feels the strength of the Lion being transferred to her. "Now you are a Lioness," Aslan says. "And now all Narnia will be renewed." Lucy believes, and her belief goes well beyond intellectual assent or even a fully engaged imagination. It transforms her will. Lucy's act of belief is the full revealing of a child of God. For this has creation been eagerly waiting. Now all Narnia will be renewed.

✳

Edmund is the first to follow Lucy's leadership. His reward is to be the first person after Lucy to see Aslan. For Trumpkin, seeing (and only seeing) is believing, but Edmund and Peter learn to see by believing first. Susan's is a more complicated case. When she first sees Aslan, she shrinks back in fear, just as the openly unbelieving Trumpkin does. But Susan never truly disbelieved. As she confesses to Lucy, her unbelief has been willful. She chose not to believe Aslan was leading them up the gorge because she was tired and wanted to get out of the woods. She didn't want to follow Aslan in the night because she wanted to sleep instead.

In *Mere Christianity*, C. S. Lewis argues that the real enemy of faith isn't reason, but emotion and imagination. Even if our beliefs are based on sound evidence, that doesn't mean we will always believe them—or always act as if we believe them. When we stop believing, it's usually because of changing moods, not a reassessment of the evidence. A child learning to swim knows the water will hold him up. It is irrational fear that makes him lose faith in his own buoyancy and sink. Faith is "the art of holding on to things your reason has once accepted, in spite of your changing moods."[8] Susan has let her changing moods overrule her belief in Aslan and her trust in the sister who has proven herself to be the group's true spiritual leader. Aslan corrects her gently: "You have listened to your fears, child." The breath of Aslan emboldens her, heals her doubt. She is ready now to take part in Narnia's renewal.

If Susan's deepest need was to have her fears comforted, Trumpkin's, it seems, is to have his fears aroused. Aslan comes to the dwarf as a conqueror first—though a benign conqueror—overwhelming Trumpkin's will.

" 'Twas grace that taught my heart to fear / And grace my fears relieved."

He may be shaking from head to toe, but Narnia's most reluctant convert is finally in the fold.

✦

Walter Hooper writes, "No, take it or leave it, men are, and always have been, inextricably bound up with the acts of God and the infinite stakes for which life is played."[9] In the end, belief and unbelief aren't about mental health or self-esteem or self-actualization. Damnation, salvation, the vast sweep of eternity are at stake when a person believes or chooses not to believe. This truth is perhaps most evident in Aslan's How, when Nikabrik's unbelief reaches its logical and horrifying conclusion. The black dwarf has finally sold his black soul. As far as the "old legends" go, he's as willing to try one as another, and since calling on Aslan appears not to have helped, he has taken steps toward calling on the White Witch. The hag and the werewolf are not only his link to the White Witch, but the very embodiment of Nikabrik's all-devouring hatred. "Nobody hates better than me," boasts the hag.

Nikabrik has left all scruples behind. His logic is characteristically specious, full of false either/or contrasts that always leave out the true option. Either the Ancient Kings and Queens didn't hear the horn, or they can't come, or they are enemies. Or, Trufflehunter adds, they are on their way. Either Aslan is dead, or he is not on the Old Narnians' side, or he is being held back by some stronger force. Or, Trufflehunter might have suggested, Aslan has sent help already. Help "may be even now at the door," the ever-faithful Trufflehunter insists. He may think he's speaking figuratively, but he's speaking the literal truth. If only Nikabrik could believe it.

The others are shocked at Nikabrik's suggestion that they call up the White Witch. But to Nikabrik she represents power, and he has narrowed to the point that he cannot care about anything else. "A hundred years of winter," he marvels. "There's power if you like. There's something practical." Nikabrik's lust for power and practicality has blinded him to the obvious fact that there is hardly anything less practical than a hundred-year winter.

And all the while, Kings Peter and Edmund are just outside the door. They have come to be Nikabrik's salvation. Instead, they are the death of him.

*

The defeat of the Telmarines is a matter of myth become fact—the Old Stories come to life. The trees and the waters awaken. And while that may be the Old Narnians' fondest hope, it is a terror to the Telmarines. "What the wicked fears will come upon him, / And the desire of the righteous will be granted" (Prov. 10:24). Sometimes, as here at the Second Battle of Beruna, what the wicked fear and what the righteous hope turn out to be the same thing. The Telmarines have made enemies of the trees and rivers, have invented stories to justify their enmity. Now that enmity comes home to them. They have pretended the forests were alive with ghosts; it's worse than they imagined: the trees of the forests are alive with a power of their own, and that power is not friendly to the Telmarines.

Some Christian readers may be troubled by the wild paganism to be found in the last few chapters of *Prince Caspian*—the river gods and forest goddesses, Silenus and Bacchus and his maenads. As Susan says, "I shouldn't have felt safe with Bacchus and his wild girls if we'd met them without Aslan." She's quite right: Bacchus and his train would be a dangerous lot indeed if they were left to their own devices. Those who don't believe it can visit Panama City some spring break and see for themselves. But Aslan *is* here, and all that wildness and freedom are an expression of the enlivening, joy-giving, creative energies of Aslan himself. What Lewis says of the God of the Bible is true of Aslan:

> It is He who sends rain into the furrows till the valleys stand
> so thick with corn that they laugh and sing. The trees of the

wood rejoice before Him and His voice causes the wild deer to bring forth their young. He is the God of wheat and wine and oil. In that respect He is constantly doing all the things that Nature-Gods do: He is Bacchus, Venus, Ceres all rolled into one.[10]

This is not polytheism that is breaking out in Narnia. The little nature gods of Narnia do not set themselves up as rivals to Aslan. They are his servants, just as Trufflehunter and the Pevensies, and now Trumpkin, are his servants.

All Narnia is renewed, just as Aslan had said it would be. The natural world is "set free from its slavery to corruption into the freedom of the glory of the children of God" (Rom. 8:21). It was the faithlessness of Sons of Adam that had enslaved Narnia in the first place. The faith of Lucy, Edmund, Peter, Susan, and Caspian has set things right again. The glory of Aslan's children is the freedom of the rivers and the trees.

Those who choose to do things their own way eventually get what they ask for: a world emptied of divinity, a life devoid of wonder. But as we believe and turn again to the Maker of Heaven and Earth, the world offers up such abundance as it has to give—not ultimate joy, of course, but gladdening echoes of it. The believer no longer looks at the world and asks, "Is this all there is?" He looks at the world and marvels, "All this, and heaven too?"

.⁕.

The story of Christ, according to C. S. Lewis, "demands from us, and repays, not only a religious and historical but also an imaginative response. It is directed to the child, the poet, and the savage in us, as well as to the conscience and the intellect."[11] Belief is wholeness. It bridges the imaginative and feeling self to the rational self. Caspian crosses the bridge from the imaginative side to the rational, first feeling the truth of the Old Stories and believing them as fact only later. Trumpkin has to cross from the other direction. Only after he is convinced of the facts can he begin to feel the awe that radiates from the Old Stories.

When a myth becomes fact—when it leaves the world of imagination and plays itself out in the world where people actually live—it makes all-encompassing claims on those who believe it. It is one thing to imagine dwarfs. As Caspian found out, it's quite another to be alone with a dwarf who might want to call you to account. It's one thing to imagine a "Dying God." It's quite another thing to come to terms with the fact that if God really did die, he requires that you take up your cross and follow him. When myth becomes fact, you are no longer the audience of the story, but an actor in it. It is one of the great mysteries: the story somehow depends on those who depend on the story.

CHAPTER THREE

Finding Self, Forgetting Self
The Voyage of the Dawn Treader

 One of the enduring images of *The Voyage of the Dawn Treader* is Reepicheep in the front of the ship, up by the dragon's head, urging the *Dawn Treader* onward, eastward toward his destiny. Indeed, it seems as if it is Reepicheep's desire, as much as the westerly wind, that drives the ship along. The smallest of the characters in the Chronicles of Narnia, Reepicheep embodies magnanimity—literally, largeness of soul. He is a mouse of vision, and his whole life is defined by the song the dryad sang over his cradle:

> Where sky and water meet,
> Where waves grow sweet,
> Doubt not, Reepicheep,
> To find all you seek,
> There in the utter east.

Reepicheep is forever looking east, seeking more and greater adventures.

It seems at times that a sense of adventure is the only sense Reepicheep has. An utter disregard for his own safety is one of the more obvious expressions of the self-forgetfulness that shapes his character. He has mastered every instinct that might induce him to turn inward, to protect himself, to draw back. He knows no fear but the fear of missing out on an adventure. Even his one vanity—his overdeveloped sense of personal honor—takes him beyond himself, forces him to turn his attention outward, upward, onward. Jesus said, "Whoever loses his life for my sake will find it" (Matt. 10:39 NIV). Reepicheep, in forgetting about himself, in refusing to hold too tightly to his life, is more alive than anyone else on the *Dawn Treader*.

The exaggerated outwardness of Reepicheep's life calls attention to one of the central ironies of *The Voyage of the Dawn Treader*: in this story of adventure on the high seas, of uncharted islands and strange creatures, the reader is struck by the *inwardness* of so many of the major conflicts. There are, of course, "real" struggles and battles—with the governor of the Lone Islands and with the sea serpent, to name two. But the most memorable struggles in *The Voyage of the Dawn Treader* tend to be characters' struggles with themselves. Eustace meets a living, breathing dragon; but the struggle turns out to be not a battle between Eustace and that dragon, but between Eustace and his own dragonish tendencies. Even in the battle with the sea serpent, the most significant moment is Eustace's act of bravery—wholly ineffectual as regards the outer battle, but demonstrating the boy's triumph over a lifetime of cowardice and self-protection.

For Eustace, the chief danger of the voyage is neither dragon nor sea serpent, neither storm nor slave trader, but his own self-absorption. His soul is in constant peril of being smothered underneath his petty self-regard. He suffers the affliction of the thoroughly selfish: in all his self-centeredness, he has lost track of himself. His only hope of finding himself is in self-forgetfulness.

That's a recurring theme in *The Voyage of the Dawn Treader*. The overweening self appears again and again—and not just for Eustace. Lucy, usually so levelheaded, falls prey to vanity as she reads Coriakin's book of spells. The Duffers are trapped inside their own self-consciousness and yet, like Eustace, they are perfectly devoid of self-knowledge. Lord Rhoop's personal hell is to be trapped deep within his unconscious, unable to live in the world outside. True freedom in *The Voyage of the Dawn Treader* is freedom from the self, freedom to turn one's attention outward, toward the things that give purpose and meaning to the self. Those who receive the gift of self-forgetfulness discover liberty. Those who will not receive it, like the Duffers, stay trapped in a prison of their own making.

Like so many other stories of great journeys, *The Voyage of the Dawn Treader* is episodic in its structure. The *Dawn Treader* carries its passengers from adventure to adventure across a world of astonishing variety. That variety, which makes *The Voyage of the Dawn Treader* such a pleasure to read, makes it difficult to write about. The different episodes vary not only in setting and character, but also in theme. This chapter, therefore, touches selectively on those episodes that best illustrate the overarching themes of self-absorption, self-knowledge, and self-forgetfulness.

✷

When we first meet Eustace Scrubb, he is not the sort of boy who would read books like the Chronicles of Narnia. "He liked books if they were books of information and had pictures of grain elevators or of fat foreign children doing exercises in model schools." Eustace is the product (and victim) of an educational philosophy that devalues imagination and emotion—debunking both the inner life and any belief in transcendence but placing uncritical faith in information, in planning and progress, in bureaucracies and systems. By way of a "very up-to-date and advanced" asceticism, his vegetarian, teetotaling, nonsmoking parents (who also wear a special kind of underwear) propose to keep all human appetites in check. But, as C. S. Lewis points out in *The Abolition of Man*, "without the aid of trained emotion, the intellect is powerless against the animal organism."[1] Deprived of spirit, Eustace cannot help but fall victim to his own basest instincts, in spite of his high-sounding talk.

Eustace is the fullest fictional embodiment of that class of educated moderns whom Lewis called "men without chests." The chest, according to the ancients, is the seat of magnanimity—largeness of soul, "emotions organized by trained habit into stable sentiments," by Lewis's definition. The head (reason) rules the belly (appetite) through the chest. So then, unless we cultivate the right feelings (Jonathan Edwards famously called them "affections"), we cannot hope to make the right choices. A human being without a chest isn't human at all, according to Lewis, for it is magnanimity that raises us above our animal beings. Men without chests like to fancy themselves intellectuals, but Lewis vehemently denies them that honor. "It is not excess of thought but defect of fertile and generous emotion that marks them out," he says. "Their heads are no bigger than the ordinary: it is the atrophy of the chest beneath that makes them seem so."[2] Eustace, true to his type, is characterized by intellectual pride, but he possesses no special intelligence.

It is magnanimity that allows the self to expand beyond

its own borders. The magnanimous grow ever larger while the small-spirited collapse on themselves. Eustace cannot reach beyond himself. He is so self-absorbed, in fact, that he can't possibly take a step back to judge his own motives, to see himself as others see him, to gain self-knowledge of any kind.

Eustace, you might say, is the anti-Narnian. He is perfectly at home in the dehumanizing atmosphere of his too-modern world. It is one thing to be resigned to life in such a world; Eustace revels in it. He has drunk deeply of the myth of Progress, and he has no interest in chivalry or honor, in tall ships or swordplay, in anything the modern world has left behind. He is the sort of boy who, offered a flagon of spiced wine, asks instead for Plumptree's Vitamized Nerve Food, made with distilled water.

Eustace's doubts about his cousins' stories are understandable. Even a person of imagination could hardly be expected to believe Edmund and Lucy's tale of Narnia if he has never seen Narnia for himself. The amazing thing about Eustace is that he can't see anything remarkable in Narnia once he gets there. His sense of wonder is so stunted that even the experience of being flung through a picture frame and into another world neither impresses him very much nor alerts him to the fact that he is in for experiences that his modern assumptions and sensibilities can't account for. His repeated demands to be taken to the nearest British consulate demonstrate how little he understands what has happened to him.

Eustace is a critic at heart. He stands far enough back from the people and events around him that he can criticize without getting personally involved in any of it. Edmund and Lucy immediately fall in love with their graceful little ship. Eustace, unaffected either by the *Dawn Treader*'s beauty or the romance of a sea voyage, boasts of the superiority of submarines and liners and motorboats, in spite of the fact that, before boarding the *Dawn Treader*, he had only been to sea once, on a very short trip, and was seasick the whole time.

Eustace lacks the one critical skill that makes it possible for a critic to be of some actual use. He lacks the ability to see anybody's perspective but his own. He stands aside from the goings-on around him, and so he believes he enjoys an objective view of things. In fact, his refusal to engage leaves him with no outside point of reference. It leads to the grossest sort of subjectivity. Because he is seasick, he is convinced that the ship must be sailing through a storm. Nothing can convince him of the truth that the weather is perfect for sailing. Nothing, in fact, can induce him to be interested in the truth, regardless of what he might say about facts and the dangers of wishful thinking. He clings to an almost psychotic version of events that corresponds only to his inner states and has nothing to do with the facts of the outer world.

As he grows more and more disaffected, he comes to believe that Edmund and Caspian, who have been exceedingly generous and tolerant, are "fiends in human form." As Eustace himself says, "One of the most cowardly things people can do is to close their eyes to the Facts."

✦

Eustace's cowardice comes into sharpest focus in his conflicts with Reepicheep; here mean-spiritedness and magnanimity are juxtaposed. Eustace likes animals, as long as they are dead and pinned to cards—in other words, as long as they are reduced to mere objects to be observed. Nothing in Eustace's experience has prepared him to meet a talking mouse, and certainly not a talking mouse who is his moral superior in all respects. Because Eustace knows nothing of courage, he believes he is safe bullying a creature so much smaller than he. Courage is a virtue no doubt debunked at the model school Eustace attends, for its basis is emotional. More to the point, courage is "emotion organized by trained habit into stable sentiment." And it is that habit, that training, that both informs Reepicheep of the proper response and steels him to carry it through in spite of the danger.

With no code of honor (or, indeed, any other code of behavior) to shape his response, Eustace runs through a series of tentative responses, none of which he manages to stick to in the face of the inexorable wrath of an injured mouse. None of Eustace's responses are noble—which is to say, he never takes responsibility for his actions. His first response at the sight of Reepicheep's sword is simply a school-marmish dismissal: "Put that thing away. It's not safe."

Reepicheep won't be dismissed. Eustace tries to make his cowardice more respectable by wrapping it in a philosophy: he's a pacifist. Reepicheep still demands satisfaction. "I don't know what you mean," says Eustace, and he is no doubt telling the truth on many levels. Still refusing to take responsibility for his own actions, he faults Reepicheep for not being able to take a joke. He finally runs away from the "birching" that he has earned, and when he takes up the matter with Caspian, he threatens to "bring an action."

This is vintage Eustace. Faced with a man—or mouse—of action, he runs as hard as his still-wobbly legs will carry him. His idea of action is the kind that is brought in a court-room. He looks to a bureaucracy, to a system, to settle a matter that could be settled quite easily by two people will-ing to take responsibility for their own behavior. The sim-plicity and clarity of Reepicheep's vision, the Narnian vision, benefits by the comparison.

The last of Eustace's run-ins with Reepicheep comes dur-ing the water shortage after the great storm. Without a chest, without magnanimity, the intellect is not only "powerless against the animal organism," it quickly becomes its accomplice. In the absence of any duty to a cause larger than oneself, the power of reasoning—or, at any rate, the power of rationalizing—is quite easily recruited to the body's party. On short water rations, Eustace (like everyone else on board) stays hot and thirsty. He believes he has a fever; he thinks, therefore, that he deserves more water than the ration allows. When he sneaks to the casks by night to steal a cup of water, it is Reepicheep who catches him. Unable to master his animal appetites, Eustace has proven to be less human than the talking animal who is worthy to guard the casks.

"They all believed *him*," Eustace complains. "Can you believe it?" Of course the reader believes it. The mouse is a person of honor. The boy is decidedly not. Eustace's journal entry about the episode is a masterwork not only of rationalization ("I would have woken the others up to ask for some [water] only I thought it would be selfish to wake them"), but also of self-deception. This is a journal entry, after all, not public testimony. Eustace seems genuinely to think he's the victim.

.✴.

But even Eustace isn't beyond mending. Merciful Aslan takes drastic measures to allow Eustace to know the truth about himself: he lets the boy become what he has been becoming all along. Sleeping on a dragon's hoard, thinking the greedy thoughts of a dragon, Eustace becomes a dragon. His new self-awareness doesn't quite come immediately. He knows there is a dragon—maybe two—mirroring his every movement, breathing smoke when he breathes, holding its breath when he holds his. Though he has read nothing of dragons, he has sense enough to be terrified. But until he sees his own reflection in the pool, he still doesn't realize that he is afraid of himself.

Upon realizing that he is a dragon, his first reaction is what a reader might expect from Eustace. He is happy to know that he is the terror of the island, invincible and rich beyond counting. He is now in a position to punish Caspian and Edmund for what he perceives as their crimes against him. But soon the greater import of his transformation begins to dawn on him. His self-imposed isolation from his fellow voyagers has come to this: banishment from the human race. Now that he has no choice in the matter, he realizes that isolation isn't what he wants after all. He doesn't want to get even with his shipmates; he wants to be friends. "He wanted to be back among humans and talk and laugh and share things." Now that he has lost his human form, he begins to exhibit the first humane thoughts and feelings we have yet seen from him.

In the Western tradition, dragons have long represented

not only greed, but also the isolation and spiritual desolation of a life devoid of relationships. A dragon's life is devoted to guarding that which cannot do him any good. No hope of happiness from his hoard, and yet a mortal fear of losing the least trinket of it—the dragon's sin (and his affliction) is jealousy even more than greed.

Pilgrim's Regress, the first book Lewis wrote after converting to Christianity, includes a song that gives voice to the misery that Eustace narrowly escapes. It is the song a dragon sings to himself, "An old, deplorable dragon / Watching my hoard." He dares not sleep for jealous watching. He is so afraid that men will come to steal his gold that he leaves his miserable post for a drink of water only once in the winter and twice in the summer. It wasn't always thus; he was once a happily married worm. But he ate his wife. A worm cannot become a dragon without eating another worm. Now, miserable and alone, he nurses his paranoid jealousy and his hatred for the men who plot to steal his treasure even though they have the truer treasures of companionship and rest.

> They make plots in the towns to take my gold,
> They whisper of me in a low voice, making plans,
> Merciless men. Have they not ale upon the benches,
> Warm wife in bed, and sleep the whole night? . . .
> They feel no pity for the old, lugubrious dragon.

There's a Eustacian quality about the dragon's complaint. The pitiless pities himself because he is shown no pity. The dragon's song ends with a self-absorbed, logic-chopping, and (more to the point) hate-filled prayer:

> Oh, Lord, that made the dragon, grant me Thy peace!
> But ask not I should give up the gold,
> Nor move, nor die; others should get the gold.
> Kill, rather, Lord, the Men and the other dragons;
> That I may sleep; go when I will to drink.[3]

It's not hard to imagine Eustace becoming that kind of dragon. But his transformation is more remedial than punitive, and he learns his lesson.

As it turns out, a dragon who is not preoccupied with guarding his treasure is quite a useful creature to have on hand. Eustace the dragon provides his companions with wild game for provisions and uproots a pine tree to serve as the *Dawn Treader*'s new mast. He offers warmth on chill nights. In short, instead of maintaining a critical distance, Eustace has at last entered into the shared life of his shipmates. It is in common purpose that Eustace finally finds fellowship with his fellows, in spite of the fact that he cannot speak a word to them in his dragonish state.

As Lewis points out elsewhere, the ability—perhaps the necessity—to face in the same direction, toward a shared goal, is the very basis of friendship. "Lovers are normally face to face, absorbed in each other; Friends, side by side, absorbed in some common interest."[4] No longer absorbed with himself, Eustace lets himself be absorbed in the same problem that his shipmates are absorbed in: getting off the island.

Only after he has become a dragon does Eustace experience anything resembling genuine pleasure. Ironically, only after he has become a dragon does he experience anything resembling genuine suffering either. The new Eustace is likeable. More than that, he likes the people around him. He understands that his shipmates have been honest and well-meaning all the time, despite his earlier views of them. He also finds that Reepicheep, once his bitterest enemy, is now his most constant friend. But along with that new knowledge of his fellows comes new knowledge of himself. "Poor Eustace realized more and more that since the first day he came on board he had been an unmitigated nuisance and that he was now a greater nuisance still." His old smugness and superiority are gone.

It is at this low point that Aslan meets Eustace. Stripped of his old conceit and self-delusion, Eustace no longer feels so self-satisfied or self-reliant. Now Aslan is ready to strip off the dragon hide—the shell of Eustace's old self—and reveal Eustace's new, regenerate humanity. The fear Eustace feels in Aslan's presence is the first sign of the awe that has been so noticeably absent in his journey so far.

Aslan commands Eustace to undress—to shed his old nature—in preparation for his baptism. Eustace manages to slough off a layer of skin, and it's a good feeling. But the dragon hide grows back before he can get into the baptismal pool. Two more times he sheds his skin, and two more times it grows back. Aslan has commanded Eustace to undress not because Eustace really can undress himself, but because he needs to see that he can't. Regeneration isn't self-improvement. Eustace has come to the end of himself. His failed attempts to undress himself have readied him to submit to the painful work that only Aslan can do. There is much work ahead for the new and improved Eustace, but at this moment—at the moment of regeneration—there is nothing to do but to lie down and let the Lion's claws do their work.

Eustace tells Edmund, "The first tear he made was so deep that I thought it had gone right into my heart." It had. His efforts at self-improvement felt good, but they were ineffectual. When Aslan strips him, it hurts worse than anything he has ever felt before. But it's the only way Aslan will give Eustace the new self that Eustace can no longer live without. The waters of baptism heal the hurt, and Eustace emerges a boy again. The cure has begun.

✦

Eustace's is the most fully developed case of self-absorption and its cure in *The Voyage of the Dawn Treader*, but two others deserve a closer look too. The first is that of Lucy reading Coriakin's book of spells. One of the most remarkable things about this episode is the fact that it is Lucy who falls victim to vanity. Lucy is the most spiritually sensitive and spiritually mature of the characters in the Chronicles of Narnia. And yet even Lucy is not immune to the sins of self-centeredness and vanity.

Lucy finds herself flipping through the book of spells for wholly noble reasons. She has shown considerable bravery coming into Coriakin's house to reverse the spell that made the Duffers invisible and thereby to save her shipmates who are being held hostage. But she is enchanted by the book of enchantments.

She lingers over the spell that would make her beautiful beyond the lot of mortals. Its accompanying pictures depict her, Lucy, chanting the spell "with a rather terrible expression on her face," then becoming a dazzling beauty—so dazzling that the real Lucy has to look away. But the book also shows the terrible effects of such beauty. Kings throughout the Narnian world fight for her, and whole kingdoms are laid waste on her account. She sees herself back in England, where she eclipses Susan, the beauty of the Pevensie family. And not only is the Susan in the picture less beautiful than the beautiful Lucy, she is less beautiful than the real Susan, and she wears a "nasty expression" on her face. She has grown jealous of her little sister, "but that didn't matter a bit because nobody cared anything about Susan now."

It's a little jarring to know that Lucy could harbor such selfish thoughts. It's even more jarring to see that Lucy, having observed the harm that kind of beauty would bring on other people, seems determined to say the spell in spite of her conscience. It's the worst sort of self-aggrandizement, this conscious wish to gain at others' expense. But Aslan intervenes. When Lucy sees the Lion's snarling face, she knows not to carry out her plan.

Aslan does allow her next act of poor judgment, however. By way of consolation for being denied beauty beyond the lot of mortals, Lucy says the spell that will let her hear what her friends think about her. This spell doesn't threaten to cause geopolitical upheaval like the last one, but it does cause considerable sorrow for Lucy. When she hears what her friends say behind her back, she learns the danger of knowing that which is not hers to know.

The next page of the magician's book, by Aslan's grace, contains a spell "for the refreshment of the spirit." It's a very different spell from the other two that have enchanted Lucy. Those spells promised her power. They put her in the position of actor, put her at the center of things. Remember the picture of Lucy, terrible in her power, chanting the beauty spell. But this spell puts Lucy in the posture of recipient rather than actor. It's more story than spell, and as she reads the story, she loses herself in it. The story-spell offers the refreshment and release of forgetfulness. Lucy forgets, in fact, that she is even reading. She is living the story; she has left her world of self-imposed sorrows. Having laid aside the will to exert her own power, Lucy is again in a position to receive Aslan's blessings.

When Lucy speaks the spell to make invisible things visible, Aslan appears. He has been there all along. And when Lucy sees him, her face is lit by a beauty like the beauty of the Lucy in the picture. True beauty comes not through the self-conscious rituals of vanity, but through the joy of the Lion. It's no minor detail that when Lucy's face does take on beauty beyond the lot of mortals, she doesn't even realize it. The misery brought on by her eavesdropping seems far away as Lucy loses herself in Aslan.

One can hardly remain self-conscious in the presence of such a terrible and joy-giving being as Aslan. Lucy "bur[ies] herself in his shining mane." She has died to self. She asks if she will ever be allowed to read the story that had so refreshed her spirit. "Indeed yes," answers Aslan, the story's Author. "I will tell it to you for years and years." For years and years she will live in a story so beautiful that she won't even bother to think about what anyone but Aslan thinks of her. That is paradise indeed.

✳

Self-absorption is distilled to its terrifying essence in the episode of Lord Rhoop on Dark Island. When the *Dawn Treader* leaves the light of day and is enveloped in an uncanny darkness, it becomes apparent that we are entering another kind of world—one that has no connection to the world of sky and wind and light. The travelers' instincts tell them to avoid this eerie place at all costs. But the voice of Reepicheep urges the *Dawn Treader* onward. He's not afraid of the dark, and he puts his shipmates in the uncomfortable position of compromising their honor if they don't plunge in.

Out of the darkness they hear the ghost-like voice of Rhoop: "Mercy! Even if you are only one more dream, have mercy. Take me on board. Take me, even if you strike me dead." When they bring Rhoop on board, his eyes are wild with terror. He urges the crew to row as hard as they can from this cursed place. This, he explains, is the island where dreams come true. And not daydreams either—not the self-flattering reveries of an idle hour. Here the dreams of sleep, the spawn of the deepest, darkest subconscious, come to life. When that realization settles on the sailors, they stop all light talk of fond hopes and fulfilled wishes and blunder through the darkness to the oar benches. Even as they pull for the light, each voyager hears the dreadful sound effects of his own pet nightmares—giant scissors opening and closing, "them" climbing up the ship's sides, gongs awakening some unknown terror.

The unconscious, that roiling factory of dreams, can be a very dark place; the veil of waking consciousness is a blessing we usually take for granted. On the island where dreams come true, Rhoop found himself living in his own subconscious, imprisoned in the deepest corridors of his mind. He got there, apparently, by his own volition. Not knowing himself, he thought he liked the idea of his dreams coming true. But it was all a trap. The neuroses of the former Eustace— the egotism, the isolation, the wishful thinking, the detachment from reality—metastasize into something resembling a psychosis on Dark Island. Rhoop could no more have pulled himself out of it than he could have pulled himself to his feet by his own belt loops.

As it turns out, the crew members of the *Dawn Treader* don't have what it takes to deliver Rhoop either. Their panicked rowing doesn't seem to be getting them very far— though in pitch-darkness it's hard to say. Beset by the suspicion that they are going around in circles, the sailors begin to despair of ever getting out of the darkness. Rhoop is convinced that it's all another horrible dream.

Not surprisingly, it is Lucy who recognizes what to do. She prays. From the darkness, where she and her shipmates have no hope of helping themselves, she calls out to the One who is light. The first help comes in the form of a peace that defies explanation. Though nothing about her outer world has changed, she begins to feel better; she views things from a more positive perspective. "After all," she thinks, "nothing has really happened to us yet." But the help of Aslan is a matter of more than just better feelings. It isn't long before a speck of light appears in the distance, then becomes a shaft of light illuminating the ship. Out of the light appears an albatross (which looks like a cross from a distance). The bird is Aslan, though only Lucy knows it, and he leads the ship out of darkness and into glorious light.

They have reentered the outer world. Rhoop himself can only stare in joy and wonder. He feels the bulwarks to reassure himself that he is really in the world of solid objects and no longer inside a dream world of his own making. He is out of himself at last, and he wants nothing more than to forget what has happened to him.

The *Dawn Treader*'s departure from Dark Island is the one section of the Chronicles of Narnia that Lewis revised extensively between editions. In the original British edition, once the *Dawn Treader* returns to the light, "all at once, everybody realized that there was nothing to be afraid of and never had been." And when they look astern toward Dark Island, it has disappeared. By the time the American edition of *The Voyage of the Dawn Treader* came out, Lewis decided that this account of the voyagers' escape made too light of their fears. He had suffered night fears as a child. In the American editions (prior to HarperCollins' 1994 edition[5]), the narrator doesn't say there was never anything to fear; rather, the reentry into the light is compared to the joy of waking in the bright light of morning and realizing that a terrible nightmare is over. And rather than disappearing, Dark Island in the pre-1994 American editions grows gradually smaller as the ship sails away from it. The terrors of the dream world are real, Lewis insisted. But they aren't as real as the "warm, blue world."

Rhoop's greatest wish is to forget, and on the *Dawn Treader*'s next stop, Ramandu is able to grant his wish. He gives Rhoop sleep, and what's more, sleep without dreams.

✦

But rest isn't the ultimate goal of self-forgetfulness. Even Rhoop, when his sleep is over, will sail back to Narnia and get on with his life. Not Reepicheep, though. His obsessive wish is for the "utter east." He will sail, then paddle, then swim if he needs to, ever eastward, ever closer to Aslan's country. "And when I can swim no longer, if I have not reached Aslan's country, or shot over the edge of the world in some vast cataract, I shall sink with my nose to the sunrise." He is the picture of pure focus. Aslan's country is his *telos*, his end, in every sense of the word: the end of the world, the end of his life, the goal and purpose toward which he bends his every effort.

Reepicheep's desire is the same desire the apostle Paul speaks of: "I press on to lay hold of that for which also I was laid hold of" (Phil. 3:12). In his single-mindedness, Reepicheep forgets everything, counts it as rubbish compared to the destiny that laid hold of him in the dryad's cradle song long before he was able to lay hold of it:

> Where sky and water meet,
> Where waves grow sweet,
> Doubt not, Reepicheep,
> To find all you seek,
> There in the utter east.

Paul continues, "Forgetting what lies behind and reaching forward to what lies ahead, I press on toward the goal for the prize of the upward call of God in Christ Jesus" (Phil. 3:13–14). That goal, of course, is heaven, the country of his true citizenship. And there in heaven, "the body of our humble state" (v. 21) will be transformed into glory—the shining brightness of perfected honor. That's what the overwhelming brightness of the sun in the Last Sea is about. It is glory, the light of Aslan's Country.

Ramandu, the gatekeeper of the End of the World, is a retired star, and every day, with every fire-berry he eats, he grows a little brighter, more glorious in preparation for his return to his place in the heavens. Every day the *Dawn Treader* sails closer to Aslan's country, the sun grows in its glory. It's a brightness that would dazzle the travelers' eyes under normal circumstances. But the brighter the sun grows, the more they are able to take in its brightness. In the Last Sea, the water itself is drinkable light. The sailors have no need for food when they drink the stuff, nor sleep either. It is life to them: "They felt almost too strong and well to bear it."

Drinking the sweet waters of the Last Sea, the travelers on the *Dawn Treader* are literally partakers in glory. But they aren't merely taking glory in; they are becoming glorious themselves. Everything about them grows more glorious. "We do not merely want to *see* beauty," Lewis writes in his sermon "The Weight of Glory." "We want something else which can hardly be put into words—to be united with the beauty we see, to pass into it, to receive it into ourselves, to bathe in it, to become part of it."[6] On earth we are always outside the beauty we observe. The glory of heaven is to shine with the same beauty that breaks our hearts on earth.

Glory in the biblical sense isn't merely brightness; it's the brightness of honor, of accolade, of good report. Reepicheep's obsessively cultivated honor is just a shadow of the honor he will exude in Aslan's Country. For the truest and highest honor is the approbation of the Judge of

Heaven and Earth: "Well done, good and faithful servant!" (Matt. 25:21 NIV).

To bask in God's approval—it may sound like the ultimate vanity. But, as Lewis argues, it is the purest, even the humblest pleasure of the creature, to please the One who made you for his pleasure. "There will be no room for vanity then. She will be free from the miserable illusion that it is her doing. With no taint of what we should now call self-approval she will most innocently rejoice in the thing God has made her to be, and the moment which heals her old inferiority complex for ever will also drown her pride."[7]

In Aslan's country, all selves will be free—and their freedom will be a freedom from the self. Eustace's self-absorption will be a distant memory as he absorbs glory and is absorbed into it. Lucy will no longer care what her friends say about her behind her back, overwhelmed instead by the loving words the Lion speaks to her face. The darkness of Lord Rhoop's inward hell will be flooded by the light of Aslan's Country. The last we see of Reepicheep, he is headed for that country, completing the journey he has pursued so long and so hard. Forgetting himself, forgetting the world, forgetting everything that lies behind, he goes up, up, up, to be welcomed into the heart of things.

CHAPTER FOUR

Remembering the Signs
The Silver Chair

 As we have seen already, the process of coming to belief is a central theme in *Prince Caspian*. Though they go about it in very different ways, both Caspian and Trumpkin the dwarf make an assessment of the evidence before they decide that the truth is true. The life of faith begins with that decision: given the evidence I have before me, I believe these things to be true.

There is yet another kind of belief at work in *Prince Caspian*. Lucy, Edmund, Peter, and Susan also have to believe before they can complete the task for which Aslan brought them into Narnia. For them it is not a question of evidence. They have been in the overwhelming presence of Aslan; there is little chance of their doubting his existence. The belief they need has more to do with trusting in a person than believing a set of propositions. *The Silver Chair* offers a fuller examination of that kind of faith—the kind that has to muddle through in a world that usually obscures the evidence that first made faith possible.

Around the same time he wrote *The Silver Chair*, C. S. Lewis wrote an essay entitled "On Obstinacy of Belief."[1] In it he draws a distinction between "the way in which a Christian first assents to certain propositions, and the way in which he afterwards adheres to them."[2] A person who accepts Christianity does so because he or she thinks there is good evidence for Christianity's claims.[3] We consider it foolish, not virtuous, to assent to any proposition without evidence—even a religious proposition.

Why is it, then, that Christians count it a virtue to stick to one's religious beliefs in spite of evidence that would seem to argue against them? Because once you believe, "you are no longer faced with an argument which demands your assent, but with a Person who demands your confidence." And when a friend has earned your trust, continued trust means (by definition) not requiring constant proof of his or her good intentions. "There are times when we can do all that a fellow creature needs if only he will trust us," Lewis writes. When you are helping a dog out of a trap, he has to trust that pushing his paw further into the trap is really the only way he can get out. When you are getting a thorn out of a child's finger, she has to trust that the pain of the extraction is the only thing that will make her feel better. "We are asking them to trust in the teeth of their senses, their imagination, and their intelligence."[4]

Aslan asks Jill and Eustace to trust him in spite of their senses, their imaginings, and even at times their intelligence. Their first task is to remember what they know to be true. But it is easy to forget. The immediate experience of the five senses, the desire for creature comforts, fear, doubt all want to have their say in the matter, and it can be hard not to give them the last word. On top of that, Jill and Eustace face the deceit of clever enemies. The central question of *The Silver Chair* is not how one comes to believe the truth. The question is how one holds onto the truth in spite of all.

⁂

Jill doesn't start out a believer. She comes to believe in Aslan when she is presented with the most irrefutable of all evidence: she meets him face-to-face. Like most people when they see Aslan for the first time, she is terrified. But she is also terribly thirsty, and the only water to be had is a stream guarded by the Lion himself. "If you are thirsty," Aslan says, "come and drink." He alone has what Jill needs. He wants Jill to have as much water as she wants, but on his terms, not hers. He will not go away while she drinks. He won't even promise not to eat her. "I have swallowed up girls and boys, women and men, kings and emperors, cities and realms," he tells her. He's good, but he's not safe.

"I daren't come and drink," says Jill. But she cannot afford not to dare. There is no other water. So Jill does the only thing she can do: she drinks from Aslan's stream. It is the coldest, most refreshing water she has ever tasted. This is living water. Now she realizes that, as dangerous as the Lion might be, running away from him would be the most dangerous thing of all.

When Jesus gave living water to the woman at the well, he confronted her with her sin. "Where is your husband?" he asked, not because he didn't know already, but because the woman needed to acknowledge that the man she lived with was not her husband (John 4). Aslan asks a similar question of Jill: "Human Child, where is the boy?" Until Jill owns up to her role in Eustace's fall from the cliff's edge— that is to say, until she confesses her sin—Aslan's water won't fully do its work on her. At first she tries to answer the Lion's questions without taking responsibility. "He fell over the cliff. . . . He was trying to stop me from falling, Sir." But Aslan insists on the whole truth. He isn't satisfied until Jill admits that it was her pride and vanity that brought her so close to the cliff's edge to start with.

When Jill confesses her sin, Aslan's aspect softens. "That is a very good answer, Human Child," he soothes. "Do so no more." Jill's sin is forgiven, and now she is ready to complete the task for which Aslan is bringing her to Narnia. That doesn't mean all the consequences of her sin will melt away. Her task will be more difficult now that Eustace has gone ahead of her. But she is not disqualified. Aslan assigns Jill a task that she couldn't possibly complete on her own. What does a twentieth-century English schoolgirl know about rescuing a lost prince? But he also gives her four signs by which he will guide her quest. He doesn't ask Jill to decipher the mystery. He asks her only to trust and obey.

After such a powerful encounter with the Great Lion— after receiving instruction from the very mouth of Aslan— it might seem that Jill could not fail to remember his words. But Aslan warns her otherwise: "Perhaps you do not see quite as well as you think." On the mountain in Aslan's Country, it is easy to believe and trust. All is clear on the mountaintop. But Jill's work is down in Narnia, and there the signs won't look the way she expects. "That is why it is so important to know them by heart and pay no attention to appearances. Remember the signs and believe the signs. Nothing else matters."

✳

At first Jill is eager to remember Aslan's four signs. Early in her airborne journey from Aslan's Country to Narnia, she dutifully rehearses the signs. The Lion's warning is still fresh. She is still high above Narnia, and everything is still clear. Jill takes comfort in her ability to say the signs correctly—too much comfort, in fact. In her complacency she falls asleep, and when she wakes her mind is on other things.

When Jill arrives in Narnia, there are so many wondrous things to take in that she doesn't even think about the signs for the first half-hour she is there. It's a crucial half-hour. Aslan's first sign requires that Eustace greet the first person he sees in Narnia, an old and dear friend, in order to receive "good help." Jill, of course, wasn't with Eustace when he first set foot in Narnia. This is the first complication resulting from Jill's boastful foolishness at the cliff's edge. Perhaps they could have still benefited from the first sign if Jill had only remembered Aslan's other warning: in Narnia the signs won't look the way she expects them to look.

Eustace doesn't recognize his friend King Caspian, who has lived through seventy years of Narnian time since Eustace last saw him. The sign specifies, "As soon as the boy Eustace sets foot in Narnia, he will meet an old and dear friend." The sign gives Eustace and Jill a way of understanding a situation that their five senses can't. But Eustace falls back instead on what he sees, and he gets it all wrong: "There's nobody I've ever seen in my life before." To understand the sign is to interpret one's circumstances in light of the sign, not the other way around. The king's ship sails before Eustace realizes who he was. Jill and Eustace have missed the first sign.

.⋆.

Three signs remain. Jill and Eustace's task would surely have been easier if they had King Caspian's resources at their disposal, but all is not lost. The signs direct them northward, and their wise (though not entirely courageous) advisers, the owls, agree that what they need is a Marshwiggle to guide them. Puddleglum seems an unlikely guide for such a high-spirited adventure as the one ahead of Jill and Eustace. The rescue of a lost prince surely calls for dash and élan—qualities noticeably lacking in the gloomy, muddy Marshwiggle who takes such a serious view of life.

Puddleglum's outward pessimism conceals a deep and abiding faith in Aslan that gives him an unshakeable steadiness. What at first looks like defeatism is in fact a peculiar kind of contentment. He is always ready to receive whatever life (which is to say, whatever Aslan) sends his way; being always prepared for the worst means his life is, for the most part, a series of pleasant surprises. Puddleglum's pessimism can also be read as a kind of humility. He never assumes that he has a right to be happy. He never feels he deserves better than what he's getting. Imagine a life free from disappointment. There is genuine freedom in such an outlook.

Puddleglum is steadiness personified. He is forever who he is, regardless of his circumstances. His outlook may seem gloomy next to Eustace and Jill's youthful enthusiasm, but when their spirits sink toward despair, Puddleglum's ever-constant temper buoys them again. His cautious nature may come across as fearful next to the children's excessive and uninformed confidence. But when they are paralyzed by fear, it is Puddleglum—no less cautious than usual, but no more fearful either—who steels them to act.

Puddleglum understands the value of suffering. Therefore he doesn't try very hard to avoid it; at any rate, he doesn't let the desire for comfort keep him from doing his duty. Perhaps that is his greatest contribution to the quest. "Now a job like this," he says, "a journey up north just as winter's beginning, looking for a prince who probably isn't there, by way of a ruined city that no one has ever seen—will be just the thing. If that doesn't steady a chap, I don't know what will." Eustace and Jill can look forward to the adventures ahead if they want to. Puddleglum looks forward to the hardship. For it is hardship, not ease, that steadies a chap.

As Jill observes, books about quests and adventures don't typically detail the mundane and decidedly unglamorous vexations of life outdoors. They talk about people living on the birds they shoot, for instance, but they don't mention "what a long, smelly, messy job it is plucking and cleaning dead birds, and how cold it makes your fingers." Lewis won't allow the reader to drift off into abstraction. By keeping the wastelands journey rooted in such sensory details as cold fingers and frost-stiffened blankets, he reminds us that *adventure* or *fortitude* or *trust* (you may plug in your own abstraction) is lived only in the world of concrete experience. "Set your mind on the things above," wrote the apostle Paul, "not on the things that are on earth" (Col. 3:2). Yet here we are; we live on the earth, not above it. Jill's first task is to remember Aslan's signs. But here in Narnia, off the mountaintop, all the pains and all the pleasures of the sensory world can make it easy to forget.

When the three travelers meet the Lady of the Green Kirtle, she is the first source of delight they have run across in quite some time. Her trilling laugh, her gay clothes, her dazzling beauty are all welcome relief from the severity of their travels across the grim wastelands. Puddleglum's stiff and suspicious manner comes across as surliness in the face of the lady's exquisite charms. Puddleglum, however, is the only one of the group who is able to see beyond appearances; his reticence saves the day.

The children are so charmed by the lady's kind manner—and even more by the prospect of warmth and ease and full stomachs at Harfang—that they don't stop to think how odd it is that such a lady should be riding out in the wilds of Giantland. As for the knight accompanying the lady, Puddleglum's precise logic looks like caviling at first. He insists that he has seen only a suit of armor, not a man. It seems ludicrous for Puddleglum to suggest that the being inside the armor might be a skeleton or "someone invisible." He appears to be projecting his own morbid fears on the situation. But as far as that goes, Jill's speculations about the knight are themselves a projection of her own false optimism and are no more grounded in logic than Puddleglum's: "I expect he was shy," she says. "Or perhaps he just wants to look at her and listen to her lovely voice. I'm sure I would if I was him."

The lady may be a witch, but the enchantment the children fall under isn't properly magical. They are under the spell of their own appetites. The desire for creature comforts—warm baths, soft beds, and hot meals—prevents them from thinking straight. The children believe the Lady of the Green Kirtle without question because they *want* to believe her. Puddleglum's low expectations save him from that particular foolishness. He's not especially attached to creature comforts, so no desire for creature comforts will induce him to go to a house of giants, even "gentle giants." He's not at all sure that a giant's idea of gentleness is the same as his. But more to the point, there is nothing in Aslan's signs about staying with giants. Puddleglum still remembers what Jill and Eustace have forgotten: Aslan is their only guide.

In spite of his better judgment, Puddleglum gives in to the wishes of the children, and the three of them hurry toward a banquet where they are on the menu. Soon they find they can think of nothing but the comforts that await them.

Their mission and Aslan's signs fade into the background as hot baths and warm meals loom larger in their imaginations. The thought of better times ahead doesn't cheer Eustace and Jill, however; it only increases their dissatisfaction with their current hardships. It's the exact opposite of the gloomy satisfaction Puddleglum derives from the belief that bad times always await him; for Puddleglum, his present circumstances are never as bad as they might be, and he finds a genuine contentment in that realization.

Before they enter Harfang, the three travelers stand in the middle of one of Aslan's signs and don't even know it's a sign. On the mountaintop Aslan had warned Jill that the air in Narnia would be thick, and that it would confuse the mind. That truth finds literal representation in the snowstorm that swirls around Jill, Eustace, and Puddleglum. The weather is an outward expression of the travelers' confused minds. The real problem isn't snow blindness, but spiritual blindness.

The second sign requires that the travelers find the ruined city of the ancient giants. But they have long since forgotten about ancient giants. The cheerful lights of contemporary giants wink in the near distance, promising the ease they have long lacked. They pay attention to the hill of squarish rocks and strange trenches only insofar as it is one last obstacle before they reach their goal of Harfang. Jill's hands are so cold, and Harfang looks so warm, that she doesn't bother to wonder why this strange spot where she's standing looks so much like a ruined city. She literally falls right into the third sign—the writing on the stone—but nothing, it seems, can wake her to the things of Aslan.

Puddleglum makes a feeble attempt to refocus on the Lion's signs. But he gets Jill's petulance in return: "Oh, come *on*! Bother the signs. . . . I'm jolly well not going to give a recitation here." The Marshwiggle's gentle prompting is no match for the cold and fatigue that have turned Jill's mind aside from Aslan. Puddleglum very nearly makes a breakthrough. He has a feeling it might be worth stopping to look around. The second sign seems to be on the tip of his tongue. But the children won't hear him. They don't have time for sightseeing; the gates to the giants' castle could close at any minute. The lights of Harfang draw them like moths to a flame.

✴

Aslan punishes the travelers' disobedience by giving them exactly what they want. They make it to Harfang and are soon warm and well fed. It doesn't take long, however, to realize that they have paid too high a price for their comfort. The Green Lady told them the truth: they are heartily welcome to the giants' autumn feast. She just didn't tell them the whole truth.

But Aslan is merciful. He intervenes in a dream, first

making Jill see the gravity of her error in not repeating the signs, then putting her back on track. From her vantage point in the window of her comfortable prison, Jill can see that the hill of the strange trenches is the ruined city of the ancient giants, and that the trenches are letters carved in the stone: UNDER ME.

Jill, Eustace, and Puddleglum each acknowledge his or her own share in the guilt; they are on the path again—spiritually, at least. They still face the challenge, however, of getting back on the path physically, geographically. UNDER ME is not so clear an instruction as they had hoped for. How does one look for a prince under a massive stone? Not even Puddleglum claims to know. He knows only that "Aslan's instructions always work: there are no exceptions." That simple statement is the pivot point of *The Silver Chair*. It comes, by the way, at the exact center of the book.

From here on out, Jill and Eustace live by a new code, following Puddleglum's example. Whatever appearances may be, however impossible Aslan's claims may seem, the Lion is ever faithful and ever true. The task of the believer is first to trust and obey. Understanding will come later, or maybe not at all. The success of the mission will depend not on the travelers' strength or wit, but on their ability to trust the Lion, who is utterly trustworthy.

※

Through considerable danger and difficulty, Puddleglum, Jill, and Eustace follow the third sign, and Aslan does make a way. They find themselves in Underland. "Many fall down, and few return to the sunlit lands." Few return because once they find themselves in the darkness, few can remember that there is a sunlit land to which they may return. Underland is a shadow world. It is a version of Plato's cave, whose inhabitants mistake flickering shadows for real objects. The curse of the Underlanders is to live at one remove from reality—the reality either of the sunlit lands or of bright Bism nearer the bottom of the world. No wonder the Underlanders are haunted by an overwhelming sadness. Even Puddleglum marvels at their gloom: "If these chaps don't teach me to take a serious view of life, I don't know what will."

In the sunlit lands, Puddleglum's serious view of life rescues Jill and Eustace from their naïvely sunny view of things. Here in the shadows, that same steadiness will deliver them from despair. The same Puddleglum who seemed such a wet blanket is now their only comfort. They are on the right path again, Puddleglum assures them. However grim things may seem, they are following the purpose Aslan has laid out for them. Puddleglum asks for no better cheer than that. "If you are on a wrong road," Lewis writes in *Mere Christianity*, "progress means doing an about-turn and walking back to the right road."[5] Whatever their feelings, the travelers are making progress now.

Even so, there on the dark sea of Underland, it becomes hard to remember that there was such a thing as sunshine. "You began to feel as if you had always lived on that ship, in that darkness, and to wonder whether sun and blue skies and wind and birds had not been only a dream." Underland is an upside-down world; the inversion of reality that has already been creeping in on the travelers from Overland finds its fullest expression in the person of Prince Rilian.

For Rilian, black is white, up is down. He believes his tormentor and captor to be his friend and patron. "She is a nosegay of all virtues, as truth, mercy, constancy, gentleness, courage, and the rest. I say what I know." But he knows nothing but lies. He doesn't know his own name, or his true country. "Rilian? Narnia?" he asks. "Narnia? What is that? I have never heard the name."

Jill, Eustace, and Puddleglum see at once that there is something wrong with the strange prince. Even so, the children are discouraged by his explanation of the third sign, the carving in the stone. It's the last remains of a giant's tombstone, he says; it has nothing to do with the children or their mission. "Is it not the merriest jest in the world that you should have thought they were written to you?" Jill and Eustace take his explanation at face value: they must have missed the sign after all. They must have been fooled into assigning significance to a mere accident. But Puddleglum remains steady and solid in his straightforward trust of

Aslan: "There *are* no accidents. Our guide is Aslan." Aslan knew when those letters were cut that they would be a sign for this very day.

Rilian received his information from the queen. That's where he gets all his information. He doesn't remember a time when he didn't live at her court. He knows he suffers under "most strange afflictions," they just aren't the afflictions he thinks they are. One hour each night he changes into a completely different person. The queen has convinced him that this is his madness. In fact, it is his one hour of sanity and clarity. His affliction is on him the other twenty-three hours of the day. This hour in the silver chair is Aslan's gift to Rilian. It is an hour of suffering, to be sure— much more painful than the life that has become the norm for him during his ten years' captivity. But the pain and loss he feels in the silver chair is his only connection to his true self and his true home. It keeps him from being lost completely to a life owned by his wicked queen.

The queen claims that Rilian will be released from his enchantment once she has made him king of Narnia. She proposes to make him a usurper of the throne to which he is the rightful heir. She has convinced him to invade a kingdom where he would be welcomed as a favorite son if only he came as himself. It's inversion on inversion, a masterstroke by the queen of the upside-down world. For Rilian would not be ruler after all, but the willing pawn of the true ruler, the queen.

Rilian's release from the silver chair is one of the richest, most satisfyingly complex scenes in all the Chronicles of Narnia. A whole welter of conflicting ideas and emotions and commitments leaves Jill and Eustace and Puddleglum unsure what to do in a moment of crisis. Then the word of Aslan comes down like a thunderstroke, burning away everything but the truth and freeing the Overlanders to act.

Before the change comes on him, Rilian makes a speech echoing the speech Ulysses made to his crew when he strapped himself to the mast to hear the Sirens' song. He adjures his visitors under no circumstances to release him from the chair while the fit is on him. He warns that he will beg them "by all that is most dreadful." He will plead. He will threaten. He will cajole. But for the sake of their own safety, they must take no pity. Jill, Eustace, and Puddleglum make a solemn promise among themselves not to touch the prisoner's cords no matter what he says.

When the change comes on Rilian, he doesn't become the monster he had told them to expect. In fact, his face looks nicer than it had before. Jill is the first to take pity on him. His words don't sound like ravings. In fact, this is the most sane he has seemed yet. His requests that they let him go sound perfectly reasonable. But Puddleglum won't be moved. He has made a promise. "Stand fast!" he says. "Steady!" Still calm, still sane, the prince pleads his case more convincingly: everything he said before the change was a lie. This is his only hour of sanity and truth, and the only possible hour in which he can be freed. But the travelers stand firm. "Steady! Steady! Steady!" The prisoner appeals to their pity and their sense of decency. Jill weakens, but Puddleglum restrains her: "Steady!" When the prince grows angry and begins threatening them in shrieking tones, the travelers feel justified in their staunch refusal to help.

Then the whole equation changes in a moment. Rilian calls out, "By the great Lion, by Aslan himself, I charge you. . . ." It's the fourth sign: the first person on their journey to ask them to do anything in Aslan's name will be Prince Rilian. It's a terrible moment for the travelers. They had promised not to untie the prisoner under any circumstances. But they had also promised to follow Aslan's signs. Do the words of the sign count if they are uttered by a lunatic?

Puddleglum has been urging steadiness on Jill and Eustace. Now he shows what true steadiness means. Aslan alone is trustworthy; Puddleglum will trust Aslan. He sees no choice but to follow the sign, even if it is spoken by a lunatic. Puddleglum doesn't believe in accidents, after all.

Does that mean everything will come out all right? Eustace asks. Puddleglum isn't sure: "Aslan didn't tell Pole what would happen. He only told her what to do." He expects (or at least claims to expect) that the prisoner will kill them all once they release him. "But that doesn't let us off following the sign." Puddleglum doesn't have any particular expectations about happiness. He probably wouldn't think much of the old hymn, "Every day with Jesus is sweeter than the day before." No, some days with Jesus, as with Aslan, are hard. But we are called to obey on those days, too, and to leave the reward to the One who calls us.

✳

Prince Rilian's release from the silver chair is not the end of his troubles with the queen of Underland, however. Having been released from her enchantment, he still has to face her as his old, true self before he can leave her dominions. And she is cunning. Her spells work not entirely from without the way, say, the White Witch's wand turned her enemies to stone. Her spells work from the inside out; the incense she burns helps the process along by making it hard for her victims to think straight, as does the music she makes. But her victims' captivity is a captivity of the mind by way of fuzzy, imprecise thinking and false logic.

Rilian confronts the queen with the truth: he knows who he is; he knows his true country is Narnia, and he means to go back there. She answers with a lie so obvious that it seems impossible that anyone could believe her: Narnia is one of those words from Rilian's ravings, but there is no such place as Narnia. Puddleglum contradicts her on the basis of his own experience. He knows Narnia because he has lived there all his life. The queen purposely misunderstands Puddleglum and mocks the idea of a country up above— "Is there a country up among the stones and mortar of the roof?"—but she doesn't feel the need to disprove his claim.

Narnia is in Overworld, Puddleglum explains, but the queen pretends she knows nothing of an Overworld either. Now Eustace argues from the queen's experience. He knows she has been to Overworld because he has seen her there. But the queen dismisses Eustace's remembrance as a mere dream.

The queen makes a mockery of each of the Overlanders' arguments as if they were illogical claims. But she never attacks their arguments with logic of her own. She depends instead on incense and music to deaden her victims' power of reasoning so that they will finally accept her claims without any logical support. Sheer repetition, not logic, gets the queen's claims into the Overlanders' heads. Jill tries hard to "remember a world with sun and sky," but it gets harder and harder as the queen's spell falls on her. "There never was such a world," says the queen. "There was never any world but mine."

The Marshwiggle fights hard against the charm. "You

can play that fiddle till your fingers drop off, and still you won't make me forget Narnia; and the whole Overworld too." Whether he ever sees it again or not, he knows it's there. He speaks of stars and the sun rising over the ocean and setting over the mountains. His lyricism awakens his fellows from their drowse. The memory of the sun begins to free the Overlanders from the queen's spell.

So she attacks the notion of the sun: "Is it a real thing, or only a word?" Rilian makes the mistake of dignifying her question with an answer in terms he thinks she might understand: the sun is like a lamp. It is round and yellow and gives light, only on a much larger scale than the lamp.

"You see?" the queen retorts. "When you try to think out clearly what this *sun* must be, you cannot tell me. You can only tell me it is like the lamp." The sun is only a dream, she insists, a dream copied from a lamp. "The lamp is the real thing; the *sun* but a tale, a mere children's story." Her victims finally find it easier to assent than to argue anymore. "There never was any sun," they chant like zombies.

Just before she falls completely under the queen's spell, Jill speaks up. "There's Aslan." But a lion, the queen convinces them, is nothing more than a cat improved by imagination. "You have seen lamps, and so you imagined a bigger and better lamp and called it the *sun*. You've seen cats, and now you want a bigger and better cat, and it's to be called a *lion*." She makes the argument of the materialist who, banishing the supernatural *a priori*, proposes to explain all sense of transcendence as an outgrowth of material causes. "Look how you can put nothing into your make-believe without copying it from the real world of mine, which is the only world."

The prince and the travelers are very nearly defeated; the queen has nearly completed the enchantment. Only Puddleglum has sufficient alertness to move. In his most triumphant act of the story, he sticks his webbed foot in the queen's fire to smother it. The pain clears his head like a whiff of smelling salts, and he remembers what he knows about the sun and the sky, and about Aslan. The smell of burnt wiggle-flesh has a bracing effect on his companions too. Maybe the queen is right, Puddleglum argues. Maybe Underland is the only world there is, and Overworld is just make-believe. "We're just babies making up a game, if you're right. But four babies playing a game can make a play-world which licks your real world hollow. That's why I'm going to stand by the play-world. I'm on Aslan's side even if there isn't any Aslan to lead it. I'm going to live as like a Narnian as I can even if there isn't any Narnia."

Puddleglum's speech recalls the concluding paragraph of "On Obstinacy of Belief." A skeptic cannot know from outside the faith, by reason, what a believer knows from inside, by acquaintance. But "the *quality* of that object which we are beginning to know by acquaintance drives us to the view that if this were a delusion then we should have to say that the universe has produced no real thing of comparable value and that all explanations of the delusion seem somehow less important than the thing explained."[6] The kingdom of Aslan is Puddleglum's pearl of great price. Not even his reason or his senses matter more. The queen's deceptions cannot win out over that kind of focus and clarity of thought.

✳

After the queen's defeat, Rilian is a new man. Or rather, he is released from his bondage to be the old, true Rilian again. His shield, the token of his identity, had been black and blank under the queen's enchantment. Now it is as bright as silver, and its device is the Great Lion. Here is Rilian's new identity: warrior of Aslan. "Doubtless," says the prince, "this signifies that Aslan will be our good lord, whether he means us to live or die. And all's one, for that." The veil has been lifted; he can see clearly now. And what he sees with his new eyes is the same thing the apostle Paul saw: "For me, to live is Christ and to die is gain" (Phil. 1:21). It's all one to Rilian, because Aslan is his good lord.

Rilian has wrestled with the evidence for the Overworld and for Aslan. Freed from the queen's enchantment, he can think rationally again, and it is his good reason that brings him back to a belief in Aslan. But adhering to that belief sometimes means adhering in spite of reason and appearances—and in spite of self-protective instincts. Rilian's confession of faith—his claim that living and dying are all one to him—might be mistaken for a kind of fatalism if it weren't for the fact that it is rooted in a relationship with a person. To believe in Aslan is to believe that his ways are higher than your ways, that your good lord knows what's best for you even when you don't. Belief puts us in the position of the child with a splinter, who doesn't understand why she should be subjected to the pain of extraction. She can only trust her father who says this short, sharp pain is the only way to make the pain of the splinter go away. And so Rilian, in spite of all dangers, can make that most Narnian of declarations: Let us "take the adventure that is sent us."

Now that Rilian has found himself, he can forget himself again. He can "bid goodbye to hopes and fears," for all his fears and even all his hopes are swallowed up by the all-encompassing hope of union with Aslan. This is what the Great Lion warned Jill about: "I have swallowed up girls and boys, women and men, kings and emperors, cities and realms." Rilian has been swallowed up, and he can't contain his joy, whatever the dangers.

Rilian, in the end, displays the attitude that has kept Puddleglum on the path from the beginning. Puddleglum bid good-bye to earthly hopes and fears long ago. Indeed, one wonders whether he ever bid them hello. The children have swung between irrational fear and irrational hope because they have found it hard to remember the promises of Aslan. The air is thick in Narnia. But Puddleglum, in his steady, competent attention to the task at hand, has never strayed from his simple confession. "Aslan's instructions always work: there are no exceptions."

CHAPTER FIVE

Up from Slavery
The Horse and His Boy

 In the first chapter of *The Horse and His Boy*, Shasta learns that his father—or rather, the man he has always called "Father"—is selling him into slavery. It's the best news of his dismal little life. For he also learns that he's no son of the mean-spirited fisherman who raised him, but a foundling, a foreigner to Calormen. Now he knows why he has always felt like a stranger and an alien in his own country: because it's not his country after all. Shasta doesn't know who he is, but he knows he isn't who he thought he was, and that knowledge is the first liberty he has ever felt.

Of the seven Narnia books, *The Horse and His Boy* is the only one in which there is no commerce between worlds. No magic rings or magic wardrobes or magic doors transport characters from our world to Narnia and back again. All the transportation in this story happens on horseback or on foot. Yet Calormen and the North truly are two different worlds: in Calormen the self is shaped by slavery; in the North, the self is shaped by freedom. And the transformation wrought in Shasta and Bree and Aravis and Hwin by their journey out of Calormen is no less profound than the transformation of any of the English children who come to Narnia. When they arrive in the North, they get new selves—or, rather, they get back the selves they had lost in the dark world of Calormen.

✳

If the thought of being sold into slavery isn't especially alarming to Shasta, it's because he is treated no better than a slave as it is. Indeed, in Calormen there is no such thing as freedom. Everyone is required to grovel to someone higher in Calormen's cruel hierarchy. The deference Shasta shows his "father" Arsheesh is nothing compared to the self-abasement Arsheesh exhibits in the presence of the Tarkaan who demands hospitality at his cottage. Calormene custom requires that he touch his beard to the ground on which the greater man stands. The fisherman owes the Tarkaan bed and board, but the Tarkaan doesn't owe the fisherman so much as a thank-you. He offers only abuse and contempt; the threat of violence underlies his every remark and gesture. But even the Tarkaan isn't as free as he looks. The great men's right to lord it over the peasants derives from their own willingness to abase themselves before the Tisroc, the man at the top of the Calormene food chain.

Learning that Arsheesh is not his father stirs an unfamiliar feeling in Shasta: hope. He could be anybody, he realizes—the son of a Tarkaan, or of the Tisroc, or of one of the gods. But even Shasta's hopes at this point show how far he has to go in his thinking. When he lets himself hope for a better future, he hopes for a good master, not for freedom. He imagines what it would be like to be a slave who wears fine clothes and eats meat every day. He goes so far as to imagine a master who will give him a chance to win his freedom in the wars. But he never imagines the possibility of never being a slave again. He has no way of imagining how good the news really is. He wasn't born at the top of the Calormene hierarchy; he was born outside of it. He was born free among free people.

Shasta could be anybody, and when the Tarkaan's horse speaks to him, it seems as if anything might happen. Bree opens a whole new world to Shasta. Horses can talk—some of them, anyway—and this one comes from a land where most animals do. Bree tells of northern lands of lush greenness, shady glens, fresh air. It boggles the imagination of a boy who has known nothing but the heat and sand of the Calormen seashore, who doesn't remember drawing a breath that didn't reek of fish. But even more mind-boggling, even more invigorating is the realization that this land of abundance is Shasta's own country. Shasta has felt the pull of the North all his life, though he never knew why. He never knew it was his true home he was longing for. He has grown accustomed to the barren land of Calormen, even if he has never learned to like it. But he was made for the abundance, the freedom of the North. Thence he came, and it is his destiny to return there.

Like Shasta, Bree is a stranger and alien in Calormen, and a slave too. But he remembers Narnia and the North. He has found it necessary to impersonate the dumb, witless horses of Calormen for much of his life, and he has picked up more of their habits than he realizes, but he has never forgotten his heritage, or his birthright of freedom. It is the birthright of every Narnian.

When Bree finally speaks, after so many years of silence, he speaks like a Narnian. He rejects the slavish speech of the Calormenes. When he mentions the Tisroc, he refuses to add the obligatory phrase, "may he live forever," as all Calormenes do. That's dishonest talk for slaves and fools, he says, not suitable for free Narnians. He insists that Shasta not talk that way either.

He and Shasta agree to treat each other the way Narnians treat each other. From the start, their relationship is based on mutual respect. Long before they leave Calormen, they leave behind Calormene ways and so find a kind of freedom before they reach the free lands that are their goal. They are friends and compatriots—not horse and master, but a horse and a boy. Indeed, the horse is clearly the leader of this adventure; there is an unmistakable note of condescension—though amiable condescension—in Bree's manner toward Shasta.

When the providence of the Lion brings the journey of Shasta and Bree together with the journey of Aravis and Hwin, it is readily apparent that Aravis, though she is running to the free lands, has no idea what it means to be free. She comprehends that being a free Narnian means nobody can make her marry the loathsome Ahoshta. But she doesn't yet realize that being a free Narnian also means recognizing everybody else's freedom and worth too. She is still proud and disdainful of the common boy who has crossed her path. Nor has she gotten used to the idea that Hwin is no longer *her* horse. She's not even bothered by the thought of the slave girl who was surely whipped for letting the little Tarkheena escape. The girl was a slave, after all, not a member of the ruling class.

Whatever her desire for personal freedom, for Aravis the old hierarchies still hold. Her sense of self derives from her position at the top of the Calormene social ladder. Shasta, when we first meet him, is limited by his place at the bottom of the Calormene hierarchy. Aravis is no less limited by her place at the top.

For Shasta, the arrival of Aravis is something of a set-back. Those first days of freedom and companionship with Bree, though physically hard, were a tonic for Shasta. He grew stronger, more confident, more capable. But in the presence of one who treats him like a slave, he begins to feel again like a slave—surly, ill at ease, lacking in confidence. He habitually assumes the worst about the Tarkheena and her motives. But if Aravis possesses many of the vices of the Calormene ruling class, she also exhibits its hard virtues. She is brave and loyal and brutally honest. She is intelligent and resourceful and a very good rider. In short, Aravis is as noble as she can be among a class of nobles that is devoid of *noblesse oblige*.

✦

There are clues from the beginning that Bree has drunk rather too deeply of the Calormene *ethos* during his sojourn in the South. He can be proud and contemptuous; his contempt for Shasta's donkey, for instance, erupts in a burst of plain horsiness—whinnying rather than speaking. He is vain of his appearance; he refuses to let his young and inexperienced rider hold on by rein or by mane. The reader may overlook these shortcomings—or forgive them, at least—early in the journey. Bree's self-confidence is crucial to the success of the whole venture, and his vanity could easily be interpreted as his way of educating an ignorant young boy in the ways of the free North. After years of hiding his true nobility, surely he can be forgiven for asserting the dignity of a free Narnian.

But when it comes time to pass through Tashbaan, the depth of Bree's vanity—and its potential for real harm—begins to emerge. He doesn't want to disguise himself as a common packhorse. His station as Calormene warhorse puts him well above a packhorse. Never mind that his true station in life—Narnian talking horse—puts him much farther above a common warhorse than a warhorse is above a workhorse. He balks at the idea of shuffling through Tashbaan, head down, laden like a common drudge. More to the point, he doesn't relish the idea of cutting off his long, beautiful tail for the disguise. He had imagined cutting a finer figure when he arrived in Narnia.

His unwillingness to humble himself represents a real threat to his reaching his larger goal. It is easier for a camel to get through the eye of a needle than for a rich man—or a self-important horse—to enter the kingdom of God. But Hwin, ever sensible and ever humble, points out that the more important thing is to get to Narnia.

Aravis has her own hang-ups when it comes to entering Tashbaan. The daughter of a provincial governor, she is used to traveling through the city in a litter carried by slaves, not slinking through like a slave herself. She has never come through the city gates without having the guards snap to attention. She has never had to press herself against the walls to make way in the crowded street for the passing litter of a Tarkaan or Tarkheena. She finds it hard to let go of the prerogatives of her status. She's still learning what it means to be free.

Shasta, on the other hand, has no difficulty acting like a slave. He has done it all his life. When a Calormene guard nearly knocks him down with a blow to the face, he hardly even cries.

Tashbaan is a place designed to display the wealth and might of the Tisroc and his Tarkaans. Gleaming palaces stand hard by the jostling squalor of the peasants in the streets. Soldiers abuse the populace for fun. Perhaps most telling is the city's one traffic law: the less important have to make way for the more important. The law does little to ease the flow of traffic, but it is very well suited to its purpose of reminding all Calormenes of their place in the social order.

Soon, however, the travelers come into contact with a whole new kind of nobility. The six Narnian lords come through the streets not in litters, but on foot. They are light-skinned like Shasta, but what really sets them apart from their counterparts among the Calormene ruling class is the openness of their manner. They speak freely, laugh easily, walk with a swinging ease. They are friendly and fearless, men with nothing to hide. Here is true nobility, true excellence, the kind that comes from the inside out and is not defined by any comparison to the weaker or lower born. These men are the loveliest thing Shasta has ever seen.

Shasta's encounter with the Narnian lords recalls the Ugly Duckling's first sight of the swans: "The duckling had never seen anything so beautiful. . . . He did not know what the birds were, or whither they flew, but all the same he was more drawn to them than he had been by any creatures before. He did not envy them in the least. How could it occur to him even to wish to be such a marvel of beauty?"[1]

Shasta, like the Ugly Duckling, is dazzled by his first sight of what he is destined to become. His imagination has just recently expanded enough to permit him to picture himself as anything better than a slave. He is not yet ready to imagine himself a prince. And yet the Narnian nobles recognize Shasta as one of them. They're mistaken as to his precise identity, of course. But they're closer to the truth than Shasta can imagine.

Shasta looks like a prince of Archenland, but he doesn't act like one; his behavior perplexes the Narnian lords. Rather than answering their questions and giving an account of himself, Shasta clams up, afraid to say anything lest he get himself into deeper trouble. King Edmund interprets his silence as an ignoble surliness—a refusal to take responsibility for his actions. And that, Edmund insists, is much more unbecoming of a prince than the act of running away. The Northerners are accustomed to the high-spiritedness that sometimes leads adventurous souls like Prince Corin into trouble. They accept that. But the code of honor that is the very basis of their freedom collapses when its adherents refuse to take responsibility for their actions, good or bad.

If the Narnians find it hard to understand Shasta's behavior, he finds it harder to understand theirs. He can see that they have nicer faces than the Calormene adults he knows, but it never occurs to him to tell them the truth or ask for their help. He's never known truth telling to be profitable, never been around adults who were helpful. For members of Calormen's lower orders, the closest thing to freedom they can experience is getting away with something—doing as they please and not being punished for it. Shasta, therefore, is in the habit of not giving up more information than he has to. Furthermore, he assumes the Narnians will kill him for a Calormene spy if they realize he's not Prince Corin. He knows only how Calormenes wield power; he has no concept of Narnian honor and fair play. The Narnians, yes, insist that he take responsibility for his actions; the flip side of that rule is that they would never hold him responsible for a situation over which he has no control.

The Narnians, of course, are in an even bigger dilemma than Shasta. Their state visit to Tashbaan is beginning to look more and more like a hostage situation. It is their honor that has gotten them into this predicament—or, in any case, it's their honor that makes it difficult to get out. They cannot abandon Queen Susan to gratify the desires of the prince. Their freedom is, first and foremost, freedom of conscience. But in Calormen, there is really only one law: the less powerful make way for the more powerful. There is no right, only might. The Narnians' commitment to doing what is right—their insistence on maintaining Susan's right to choose a husband for herself—has put them on the wrong side of a might that can overwhelm not only their little delegation, but all of Narnia.

Shasta's stay among the Narnians is cut short by the arrival of the true Prince Corin, his alter ego. When Corin climbs in the window, Shasta gets his first look at what he might have been in other circumstances—what he might be yet. Shasta has been conditioned his whole life to be passive, to do as he's been told. His early experiments in freedom have been a little tentative. Corin, on the other hand, is a man of action. When he climbs in the palace window, he is bloody and muddy from fighting; he sports a black eye, a missing tooth, and torn clothes. He's not merely a ruffian, however. His fight was a fight for Queen Susan's honor, which is what's at stake for all the Narnian delegation.

Corin clearly has more honor than good sense, but it's hard not to like him. Shasta has hidden the truth of his situation from the Narnians; in Corin he sees a confidant. When Shasta observes that Corin will have no choice but to tell the truth about his escapade, Corin's angry reaction is telling: "What else do you think I'd be telling them?" There is no question of getting away with anything in the code of honor shared by the Archenlanders and Corenwalders. The noble are answerable to themselves. For the prince of Archenland, telling the truth, taking responsibility is such an ingrained habit that it seems the only possible course. Shasta arrives at the right conclusion eventually, but he lacks Corin's advantages of upbringing.

Corin gives Shasta a vision of a better self, a freer self. When Corin first climbs in the window, Shasta gives an account of himself that reflects a lifetime of slavery: "I'm nobody." By the time Shasta climbs out the same window a few minutes later, he is friends with the crown prince of Archenland; he is admired for his adventurous spirit by a boy who truly knows the meaning of adventure. And that's just the beginning of what Shasta will learn about himself.

✦

By the time Shasta reaches Tashbaan, he has long since said good-bye to his old life as a Calormene. There was precious little to remember fondly, after all. Not so for Aravis. Her sense of self is still very much bound up with the trappings of aristocracy, with the privileges of the ruling class. Even if she has good reasons to run away, her first glimpse of Tashbaan reminds her of many reasons to stay. If Shasta's experiences in Tashbaan are a first hello to a Narnian way of life, Aravis's experiences are a last good-bye to the life of Calormene nobility. She has had a taste of freedom, and that freedom gives her a new way of looking at the familiar things and people of her old life. It isn't long before Tashbaan and all its luxuries lose their allure for Aravis.

Just as Corin gave Shasta a glimpse of what he might have been, Lasaraleen gives Aravis a look at the life she, Aravis, would have had to look forward to if she had followed the path her father had laid out for her. Lasaraleen embodies the superficiality and emptiness of the luxurious life of Calormene nobility. In spite of Aravis's dire circumstances and dire need, Lasaraleen can hardly bring herself to speak of anything besides clothes. She appears to have no inner life. She cannot understand why Aravis wouldn't want to marry Ahoshta Tarkaan who, after all, is one of the most powerful and wealthy men in all of Calormen. Aravis can't stand the sight of the man, who is old enough to be her grandfather, but Lasaraleen sees only the palaces and pearls that Ahoshta can provide.

It isn't long before Aravis realizes that her travels with Shasta and the horses—grueling and dirty, but free—are preferable to the luxuries of the palace life. She comes to an even more important realization: she'll be a nobody, no more important than Shasta, when she gets to the North. And that new status is something she embraces. She has taken a big step toward understanding what it means to live in a free country, and for the first time she values freedom above her high station in life. Her new self is taking shape.

Aravis's last look at the life she's leaving behind is the secret meeting between the Tisroc, Prince Rabadash, and her fiancé, Ahoshta Tarkaan. Dressed in ostentatious costumes (the least jewel on the Tisroc's robes is worth more than all of the Narnians' accoutrements put together), the Calormenes manage to be both ludicrous and terrible at the same time.

Ahoshta Tarkaan may be Grand Vizier, but he is required to humiliate himself before the Tisroc in much the same manner the fisherman Arsheesh abased himself before the Tarkaan who came to his door. He speaks to the Tisroc from his hands and knees. When he is not speaking, he touches his face to the ground, exposing his hindquarters to kick after kick from Rabadash. He absorbs an almost uninterrupted stream of insults from the Tisroc and his son.

Though Rabadash pretends the departure of the Narnians is a matter of state, what's really at stake is his personal desire to possess Queen Susan. The lives of Calormen's soldiers are his to throw away in pursuit of a woman he describes as a "false, proud, black-hearted daughter of a dog." Besides demonstrating how little he thinks of Queen Susan as a person, the speech of Rabadash demonstrates how thoroughly he is enslaved to his own passions. "But I *want* her," he cries. "I must have her. I shall die if I do not get her."

The Tisroc, for his part, isn't especially interested in his son's love life. He's not even especially interested in possessing the land of Narnia *per se*, convinced as he is that the place is inhabited mostly by demons and monsters and overruled by a chief demon in the shape of a lion. But he cannot abide the thought of a free country, especially one so small and so close to the borders of his empire. Such is the life of a Calormene. Everyone from a lowly fisherman to the Grand Vizier has to grovel—the Grand Vizier even more so than the fisherman. And the Tisroc, the one Calormene who doesn't have to grovel, is miserable and cannot sleep at night because he knows there is someone somewhere who doesn't have to answer to him.

The whole scene is reminiscent of the language of Screwtape, C. S. Lewis's fictional devil: "To us a human soul is primarily food; our aim is the absorption of its will into ours, the increase of our own area of selfhood at its expense."[2] The rituals of the Tisroc's court aim at the destruction of all sense of self and its absorption into the ego of the Tisroc. Calormen's foreign policy, too, depends on the absorption of all other countries, increasing Calormen's area at the expense of the little kingdoms on its borders.

Rabadash is convinced that any controversy that might arise over the kidnapping of Queen Susan would soon blow over. Besides the fact that the Narnian army couldn't hope to enforce Peter's will against Calormen, Rabadash believes that the prudent and wise King Peter won't fail to see the "honour and advantage" in being connected to the house of the Tisroc. He is wrong, of course. No true Narnian would see honor or advantage in an alliance bought at the price of Queen Susan's freedom.

Here we meet again one of the fundamental ironies of *The Horse and His Boy*: the Narnians are as free and open as they can be, yet the Calormenes never manage to understand their motives. The Calormenes speak of honor—they have rules about bravery in the face of death, for instance—but in the end, this code of honor is just papered over a barbaric and bloody system of power politics. The Calormenes cannot understand any honor that truly motivates one's most important decisions, and they certainly can't conceive of any honor that calls the powerful to give up their prerogatives or to use their authority for anything other than self-gratification.

"Act as free men," says the apostle Peter, "and do not use your freedom as a covering for evil, but use it as bondslaves of God. Honor all people, love the brotherhood, fear God, honor the king" (1 Pet. 2:16–17). For the Tisroc, *free* means only "idle, disordered, and unprofitable," and therefore hateful. He doesn't grasp the fact that freedom—as long as it is not used as a covering for evil—can be the basis of an orderly and just society where all are honored, even the king. A society based on genuine freedom—where everyone is not only free to answer to his or her own conscience but required to—makes for much more order and productivity than that traffic jam of a society where the only law is that the weak make way for the strong.

The Calormenes, for all their secrecy and cultivated mystery, are quite transparent in their motives. They act only out of greed and fear. The conversation among the Tisroc, the prince, and the Grand Vizier is a complex dance of greed, fear, and feigned deference. The Grand Vizier, who has the most to fear, gets his way by playing on the greed of his superiors. He succeeds in urging his enemy Rabadash toward likely death or imprisonment in the North, and in securing the Tisroc's permission for the endeavor. Yet the risk to Rabadash is of no great concern to his father. As the Tisroc says, he doesn't love his eldest son nearly so much as he loves the power and glory of his own throne. Besides, Rabadash is one of nineteen sons. For a Tisroc, a son is no less expendable than any other human life.

The last Aravis sees of her intended husband, he is crawling backwards on his hands and knees out of the Tisroc's presence. If Aravis had any lingering doubts about leaving Calormen, they are gone now. When she mentions the Tisroc, she doesn't bother to add "may he live forever." That's slaves' and fools' talk; she's headed toward freedom.

Lasaraleen, however, remains perfectly Calormene in her thinking. Her interpretation of the scene she and Aravis witnessed—of Ahoshta Tarkaan in particular—is very different from that of Aravis. Where Aravis saw a "hideous groveling slave," Lasaraleen saw a great man and a worthy husband. With no great difficulty Aravis bids good-bye to her old friend, leaving her to her lovely dresses and her lovely house. For the reader, as for Aravis, the relief is palpable as the young Tarkheena casts off from shore and leaves Tashbaan behind.

✷

When the four travelers begin their race across the desert, the hard work of freedom begins in earnest. Their flight toward freedom will be meaningless if they don't get to Archenland ahead of Rabadash and his two hundred horsemen. Freedom carries many benefits, but ease and leisure are not among them.

As the grueling work of desert travel erodes their willpower, it becomes apparent that Bree has reached his limit as the leader of this expedition. To this point, Bree has provided much-needed leadership, not to mention invaluable knowledge of the country, that has allowed them to come as far as they have. One of the great chargers of the Calormene cavalry, it is only natural that he should take charge. But they have reached a place in their journey that requires something that goes beyond Bree's training and discipline. Bree's discipline has always been external. Now the will to continue has to come from inside, and it just isn't in him. He has spent most of his life impersonating a dumb, witless horse. Now that he finally has a chance to be himself, a free talking horse of Narnia, he cannot rise to the occasion. He has a snack and a drink while his eager companions wait. And all the while, Rabadash and his two hundred horsemen thunder toward Archenland.

John Milton wrote of "real and substantive liberty, which is rather to be sought from within than from without, and whose existence depends not so much on the terror of the sword as on sobriety of conduct and integrity of life."[3] It is the meek and humble Hwin who steps up and demonstrates the "integrity of life" that will lead the travelers to full liberty. She is not a great warhorse. She lacks Bree's strength and endurance and training. But she is a wiser horse than Bree. "I feel just like Bree that I *can't* go on," she says. "But when horses have humans (with spurs and things) on their backs, aren't they often made to go on when they're feeling like this? And then they find they can. I m-mean—oughtn't we be able to do even more, now that we are free? It's all for Narnia."

Bree makes excuses rather than doing his duty. Worse than that, he cloaks his excuses in the language of superiority: wouldn't a veteran warhorse know more about forced marches than a mere riding mare? Bree is still thinking like a Calormene; he fails the friends who look to him for leadership. When they do finally get moving, it is Hwin, the weaker of the two horses, who leads the way.

Still Prince Rabadash and his two hundred horsemen charge northward, never slacking. They have spurs and whips, after all. Soon after the four travelers enter Archenland, the Calormenes come into sight behind them. At last the two horses run with all their might. Or almost: "Both horses were doing, if not all they could, all they thought they could, which is not quite the same thing." Just when all seems lost, Aslan intervenes with an act of terrifying kindness. The same roar that first brought the two pairs of travelers together echoes from very close behind them. The horses, finding their last reserves of strength and speed, fly in terror from the Lion's roar. It becomes immediately apparent that Bree has a lot more left than Hwin; he outdistances her easily.

Throughout the Chronicles, the appearance of Aslan often reveals who people really are. And it's usually not who those people think they are. When Aslan appears, claws outstretched, hot on Hwin's flanks, Shasta shows a courage and nobility that he didn't know was in him. He is unable to get the terror-stricken Bree to turn around and come to the aid of Hwin and Aravis. So he jumps from the saddle, very much to his own peril, and runs back toward the Lion. Shasta is weaponless. He is dwarfed by the Great Lion. But he faces him down nevertheless, shouting and waving his arms. It's like something Prince Corin might do. It's the last thing a Calormene slave might do.

The Hermit's cloister means rest and safety. But not for Shasta. By facing down the Lion, he has proven that he is the true leader of this adventure, and being the leader, it is his responsibility to finish out the mission even if the others cannot go on. Between Aravis's injury and the horses' now-total exhaustion, he truly is the only one who can continue. When the Hermit gives Shasta the crushing news that he must not rest but run straight to King Lune, he makes no excuses and asks only one question: "Where is the King?" He is a man of action and a man of honor. He runs to do his duty.

Shasta isn't the only one who gains self-knowledge with the appearance of Aslan. Bree, too, finds out he's not who he thought he was, and in his case the news is appalling. Living and working with dumb horses has given Bree an exaggeratedly high opinion of himself. He is unusually brave and clever compared to the company he has always kept. But now it seems likely that he won't stack up so well against the free and the brave of Narnia. Once he realizes his failure, his first thought is to go back to Calormen and submit himself again to slavery, the only life for which he feels he is fit. Bree believes that by disgracing himself, he has lost everything. For a person whose whole sense of self depends on being superior to everyone around him, it feels like an unsupportable loss when he realizes that he isn't. But for Bree, that painful realization is the only thing that can make him free; only his pride is keeping him from Narnia.

The wise Hermit speaks wisdom to Bree: "My good horse, you have lost nothing but your self-conceit." If Bree is truly humbled, he will be able to see that he isn't really as great as he thought he was, but not an irretrievable failure either. As important as it is, even honor isn't everything. True humility is not a low opinion of oneself, but self-forgetfulness. The self-consciousness of the chastised is a self-centeredness that can be as dangerous as any other kind of self-centeredness. Aravis, Tarkheena of one of the greatest families of Calormen, has already come to terms with the fact that she may be nobody special in the free North. It is a very freeing notion for her. If Bree can accept it, too, he has a decent chance of being happy and good in Narnia.

Meanwhile, Shasta encounters Aslan again. Mired in that emotional letdown, that loss of purpose that so often comes with the completion of a long and difficult mission, he thinks of Bree and Hwin and Aravis snug in the Hermit's house, and how long it's been since he has rested or eaten, and he begins to indulge in self-pity for the first time in this story. He begins, in fact, to believe that he is the most unfortunate boy in the world.

"Tell me your troubles," says Aslan from the fog. It's one of those moments when the great terror of Aslan is overcome by his even greater compassion. Very few people have shown any interest in Shasta's sorrows or fears or hopes. But this mysterious, giant voice in the fog does. Shasta tells of his difficult childhood, of his harrowing escape from Calormen, of the trouble he has had with lions.

The voice in the fog offers a different perspective on Shasta's misfortunes: they weren't misfortunes at all, but part of a larger plan. The lions on the road, the lion among the tombs outside Tashbaan, the lion who attacked Aravis, even the lion Shasta doesn't remember—the one who pushed baby Shasta's boat to shore at the Calormen fishing village—were all the same Lion. All of Shasta's life has been lived under the protective paw of the Lion: the same Lion who now speaks from the fog.

When Shasta asks who is speaking to him, he gets more or less the same answer Moses got from the burning bush: "Myself. . . . Myself. . . . Myself." Shasta has been speaking to the great I AM. He is no longer afraid, but still he trembles. He feels glad, too, in this awesome presence. Then a light dissolves the fog, and Shasta sees the Great Lion to whom he has been talking. He is more terrible and more beautiful than anything Shasta has ever seen.

Shasta has never even heard the name *Aslan*, but when he sees the Great Lion he knows exactly who he is. He drops to the ground at Aslan's feet. At first blush, Shasta's genuflection looks similar to the forced worship required by the Tisroc. That's because this spontaneous worship is the original of which the rituals in the Tisroc's palace are a grotesque counterfeit. The Tisroc's men struggle to find appropriately flattering words to say as they grovel at his feet. Shasta says nothing, knows that he doesn't have to say anything. In the Tisroc's palace, the worshipers' sense of self is obliterated, subjugated to the ego of the Tisroc. In the worship of Aslan, Shasta's self comes into full flower. The One who calls himself "Myself" has come to make it possible for Shasta to find himself, to become the self he was born to be. The fragments of Shasta's unhappy life are being put together into a mosaic of exquisite beauty.

Screwtape marvels at the kind of love that his great enemy God shows to his people, and at the free worship by which believers both lose themselves and find themselves:

> One must face the fact that all the talk about His love for men, and His service being perfect freedom is not (as one would gladly believe) mere propaganda, but an appalling truth. He really *does* want to fill the universe with a lot of loathsome little replicas of Himself—creatures whose life, on a miniature scale, will be qualitatively like His own, not because He has absorbed them but because their wills freely conform to His.[4]

Full freedom, Shasta discovers, is the freedom to worship the One who deserves worship, and the freedom not to worship anyone or anything else.

The sun is up, the fog is gone, and Shasta realizes he's in Narnia, on the other side of the Anvard Pass. The abundance of the place embodies the abundance of the new life Shasta has found after his encounter with Aslan. In contrast to the Calormene desert, the natural world in Narnia is fairly bursting with life, even intelligence. Shasta meets talking animals and dwarfs. He is welcomed and fed and introduced to such novelties as bacon and toast and butter. He's in a new and better world.

＊

Aslan makes his next appearance at the Hermit's cloister. Bree, it seems, has not quite taken the Hermit's words to heart. He is just a few miles away from Narnia, his goal in this long, arduous journey, and yet he still hesitates to go. A chief concern is his ragged appearance: he's still more interested in making a good impression than in entering fully into the life of a free Narnian horse. He rationalizes ("I have a proper respect for myself and for my fellow horses, that's all"), but in the process of rationalizing his vanity, he only exaggerates it. He launches immediately into a monologue about the nature of Aslan. It's a topic he knows nothing at all about, but he doesn't let that keep him from pontificating in a very superior tone.

His speech is interrupted by the arrival of Aslan himself. Terrified at the sight of the Lion he had spoken of as a mere figure of speech, Bree looks no less ridiculous than Rabadash will soon look. If not for the high wall enclosing the Hermit's cloister, Bree would have run away from his only help. Not surprisingly, Hwin is the first of the group to respond to the Great Lion appropriately. Always humble and retiring, Hwin has perhaps a shorter distance to go than any of her fellow travelers. She is shaking all over, but she goes toward Aslan, not away from him. "Please," she says. "You're so beautiful. You may eat me if you like. I'd sooner be eaten by you than fed by anyone else."

One wonders if Lewis had a copy of *The Ugly Duckling* open as he wrote this story of transformation, of coming into one's own. When the duckling finally goes out to meet the swans, he is convinced that they will kill him for his boldness. "But it doesn't matter," he says. "Better to be killed by them than to be snapped at by the ducks."[5] Hwin's boldness, like the Ugly Duckling's, is rewarded. Aslan promises her joy.

Next Aslan summons Bree. The great warhorse hesitates, but Aslan insists: "Do not dare not to dare." Face-to-face with the Great Lion, Bree finally demonstrates some self-knowledge: "I'm afraid I must be rather a fool." It is all he needed to say. He is ready now to be the free Narnian horse he was meant to be.

Aslan turns last to Aravis. He wants to be sure she knows that he was the Lion who dragged his claws across her back.

Those ten stripes on her back are equal to the ten lashes received by the slave girl whom Aravis drugged in order to make her escape from her father's house. If Aravis is to live free, she must sharpen her skills of empathy. She needs to know what the slave girl's lashes felt like.

Soon after Aslan's departure, another visitor comes to the Hermit's cloister: Prince Cor of Archenland. He is Shasta, who at long last knows who he really is. He is the lost son of King Lune. He hasn't yet learned the finer points of royal etiquette, and he's still quite embarrassed by the trappings of royalty, such as fine clothes and personal trumpeters. But this is what he was born for. He can now look back on his dismal little life in Calormen and see the hand of Providence. Aslan has been behind all this, he sees, and even his years of drudgery under Arsheesh were a preparation for the life he now leads.

*

There is one character in *The Horse and His Boy* whose self-revelation does him no good. Rabadash has ample opportunity to acknowledge that he is a fool and to mend. But he chooses not to. The lords of Narnia and Archenland treat him with remarkable clemency. They give him good food and comfortable lodgings. But he refuses to eat and will not sleep. King Lune is too kindhearted to execute Rabadash for his crimes (though all agree that killing Rabadash in battle would have been both a pleasure and a convenience). Instead, they agree that they will let him go free if he promises not to commit such treachery again.

Rabadash, however, refuses to hear conditions, merciful or not. He insults and threatens the men who have it in their power (and, more to the point, within their rights) to put him to death. He will not receive such grace as is offered to him.

To insult the grace of men is crime enough. When the Great Lion appears and repeats the kings' offer, Rabadash openly defies the grace of Aslan too. The prince has grounds for neither pride nor anger. He has suffered no inconvenience that he has not brought on himself (and has been spared a great many inconveniences that he might have suffered). All he has to do is to accept the proffered mercy of the northern kings. "Your doom is near," Aslan warns, "but you may still avoid it." Rabadash does nothing to avoid his doom but rushes headlong into it.

He begins making the ludicrous faces with which he intimidates his subjects in Calormen. He rolls his eyes, stretches his mouth into a grimace, wiggles his ears. But free people aren't intimidated by the same things that intimidate slaves. The shrieks and curses of the Calormene prince fill the air, but Aslan answers with the quiet voice of genuine authority: "The doom is nearer now."

Rabadash, who can stand torture or death or anything

but being laughed at, continues to make himself a laughing-stock. He has chosen his doom. His wiggling ears grow long and furry, and he becomes a donkey, the very personification of the ridiculous. His change is reminiscent of the transformation of Eustace into a dragon in *The Voyage of the Dawn Treader*. Rabadash becomes what he was making of himself already.

✦

There yet remains one more revelation for Prince Cor, formerly known as Shasta. He is not merely a prince of Archenland. He is the crown prince, twenty minutes older than Corin and heir to King Lune's throne. He doesn't seek out such honor. He hasn't fully comprehended the fact that he is free, much less a prince and a king's heir. But, as King Lune points out, Cor's feelings and desires—or anybody else's—have little to do with the matter. As elder brother, he is crown prince by law.

Cor is to be a king over free people. That is a very different thing from being a Tisroc. Corin rejoices to be free of the burden of kingship, and he has good reason. The king of a free people has more responsibility toward his subjects than his subjects have toward him. He uses his authority to secure a safe and happy life for those who submit themselves to his authority. To be a king of free people is "to be first in every desperate attack and last in every desperate retreat, and when there is hunger in the land (as there must be now and then in bad years) to wear finer clothes and laugh louder over a scantier meal than any man in your land." In short, a king over free people conducts himself in much the same way Cor has learned to conduct himself in his journey up from slavery.

To come face-to-face with Aslan is to realize that you aren't who you thought you were. That's always good news, even when it doesn't seem so at first. Status is not self. When Aravis willingly gives up her status, she gets a self in exchange. She gets freedom. Bree, for his part, finds out he's a fool. But his self-conceit was keeping him out of Narnia; to lose it was no loss at all. And Shasta, the Ugly Duckling of the story, learns that the persecutors who made his life so miserable were only barnyard fowl snapping at a swan who was destined to soar far above them.

CHAPTER SIX

Adventurer and Magician
The Magician's Nephew

 At the center of *The Magician's Nephew* is the creation of a world—the Great Lion Aslan singing
Narnia to life. And it is good. It is a world bursting with life,
a feast for the senses and a tonic to the imagination. Stars
sing. The sun seems to laugh for joy. Trees burst forth in answer to the Lion's song. Panthers and elephants and frogs
boil up from the earth, newborn and yet fully formed. And
in the middle of it all is the Creator, striding back and forth
across his creation. Here amid this riotous, teeming abundance, it's not hard to imagine Aslan making it all for his
own pleasure, and for the pleasure of his creatures.

By allowing the reader to watch the creation of another
world, C. S. Lewis evokes an appropriate awe and delight in
the things of *this* world. The Narnian perspective rejects a

materialist vision that reduces "reality" to the physical, earthbound facts of a matter. There is a Supernature that is prior to and, in fact, more real than the physical world we see around us. But Lewis never rejects the physical world as being evil *per se*. No, when God made the world he declared it good, and even in its fallen state, it offers an abundance of good and proper pleasures.

A properly Christian view of things requires more than a right relationship to the things of heaven; it requires a right relationship to the things of earth too. Your view of how the natural world relates to the supernatural determines a great deal about your religion. You might say it *is* your religion. A worldview that no longer stands in awe at the idea of creation—even if it acknowledges God's creative work as a fact—is poor indeed. *The Magician's Nephew* demands that the reader see the physical world as a *created* world. It demands that the reader respond to the creation, and to the Creator.

The characters in *The Magician's Nephew* respond to the natural world in two main ways: the way of the magician and the way of the adventurer. The magician's impulse—shared by Uncle Andrew and Jadis—can be defined as the drive to manipulate Nature for one's own ends, to direct Nature's life-giving powers toward purposes for which they were never intended. The result is a spoiled nature—what Christians have always called the Fall—and a narrowing of the self that leaves the wicked unable to open themselves to the happiness they had set out to acquire.

One of the central ironies of *The Magician's Nephew* is that in a world so thoroughly and delightfully magical, both of the villains are magicians. Good magicians appear elsewhere in the Chronicles (Dr. Cornelius in *Prince Caspian*, Coriakin in *The Voyage of the Dawn Treader*), but here at the founding of Narnia, the very essence of evil is the impulse to wield magical powers.

The opposite of the magician—in *The Magician's Nephew*, at least—is the adventurer. Seeking power, seeking to assert the self, the magician gets narrower and narrower until there is finally no self to assert. The adventurer, by contrast, is forever expanding and broadening. Rather than manipulating the created order, the adventurer opens himself to experience it. And since the world is full of surprises, the adventurer is always open to uncertainty, always ready to "take the adventure that Aslan sends us." For Lewis, adventure is a picture of abundant life. Freed from the all-absorbing selfishness of the magician, the adventurer is open to receive the blessings that life has to offer.

Digory and Polly are adventurers by nature. And in *The Magician's Nephew*, their horizons are expanded far beyond what they would have believed possible. The spirit of adventure literally opens a whole new world to them. But Digory and Polly's adventure starts very much in this world.

Digory, when we first meet him, is the very personification of earthbound sorrow and helplessness. His face is grimed not merely with earth, but with earth mixed with tears— tears shed for his dying mother and his absent father. What's more, he's a stranger in the city, alienated from his country home, where he has a pony and a river at the bottom of the garden. He's a little Adam, laid low by the aftereffects of the Fall.

But fortunately, he and Polly haven't outgrown the ability to invent imaginary worlds. In Polly's imaginary "smuggler's cave," their adventures begin in earnest. One of the first principles of the adventurer is that what looks to be a small adventure can become quite a large adventure without warning. That very uncertainty is fundamental to the nature of the thing. In the Chronicles, a flight of fancy can quickly turn into a matter of eternal weight. When Polly opens the attic door, the children's imaginary adventure is swallowed up by a much greater adventure—one in which the stakes are life and death, and ultimately the happiness of a whole planet for a thousand years and more. Behind that door, instead of a clutch of imagined robbers, they find something much more sinister: a real magician.

When we first glimpse Uncle Andrew, he is described as looking "like a pantomime demon coming up out of a trapdoor." Then, still behaving more like a stage villain than a sane adult, he locks the children in his lair and fixes them with a terrifying smile that shows all his teeth. This first impression is an important thing to bear in mind, for it won't be long before Uncle Andrew will seem laughable and even pitiable. But the fact that he's a fool and a laughingstock doesn't change the fact that his motivation is fundamentally demonic. As Lewis goes out of his way to show, Uncle Andrew is of the same cast of mind as Jadis. He does less harm than Jadis only because he has less power.

For Uncle Andrew, as for any other wicked magician, everything in the world—including the people—is an object to be manipulated. His attitude toward Polly and Digory is no different from his attitude toward his guinea pigs. They are there for his use, subjects for his experiments. As Digory rightly observes, that's not even the right attitude toward guinea pigs. Digory has had a guinea pig for a pet. That is to say, he has had a relationship with a guinea pig; he can no longer look at a guinea pig as a mere object.

Digory has a relationship with Polly, too, and while Uncle Andrew congratulates himself on the success of his experiment, Digory worries about the friend who has disappeared to who knows where. Digory is the voice of common decency. But Uncle Andrew has no use for common decency. He has convinced himself that he is beyond moral categories. People in general ought to keep promises and tell the truth, of course, but that kind of conventional morality couldn't possibly apply to "profound students and great thinkers and sages." It is right and necessary that people should make sacrifices for others—just not people like Uncle Andrew. "Men like me," he says, "who possess hidden wisdom, are freed from common rules just as we are cut off from common pleasures. Ours, my boy, is a high and lonely destiny."

It's true enough that Uncle Andrew and men like him are cut off from common pleasures. But that's no grounds for sympathy; his "lonely destiny" is one he has chosen for himself. If he is cut off from common pleasures it's because he has cut himself off. It doesn't follow that he is therefore cut loose from the common rules. A woman who has murdered her husband can hardly beg the court's mercy on the grounds that she's a widow.

It is worth noting how much the magician resembles a scientist in this scene. Uncle Andrew speaks of his magic as "experiments" performed on "subjects." He follows a version of the scientific method, coming up with hypotheses and testing them. He produces the magic rings by technical means, not by waving a wand or saying incantations. If it strikes a reader as strange to equate magicians and scientists, it was the most natural thing in the world for Lewis. He had no quarrel with pure science (he called it "natural philosophy")—the pursuit of knowledge, understanding, even appreciation of the natural world and its processes. But he was very suspicious of applied science. Applied science, he argued, takes an interest in knowledge only as a means of putting Nature to work for human beings. He writes in *The Abolition of Man*: "For the wise men of old the cardinal problem had been how to conform the soul to reality, and the solution had been knowledge, self-discipline, and virtue. For magic and applied science alike the problem is how to subdue reality to the wishes of men."[1]

Applied science, like magic, is about power, however much both disciplines talk about knowledge. And such power comes at a high price. "It is the magician's bargain: give up our soul, get power in return. But once our souls, that is, our selves, have been given up, the power thus conferred will not belong to us. We shall in fact be the slaves and puppets of that to which we have given our souls."[2]

As Uncle Andrew pontificates, it becomes obvious how fully he has entered into this magician's bargain. He is a soulless man. Everything that makes a being human—empathy, integrity, courage, a sense of justice—has withered in him. And so he is no longer able to see the humanity in other people.

Digory is nearly taken in by his uncle's high-sounding speech and the "grave and noble and mysterious" look on his uncle's face. But then he remembers another look he saw on Andrew's face: the eager, greedy look that came over him right before Polly took the yellow ring. Common sense prevails, and he sees through to the truth. " 'All it means,' he said to himself, 'is that he thinks he can do anything he likes to get anything he wants.'" That kind of moral clarity and simplicity always carries the day in the Chronicles of Narnia. The convoluted reasoning of sophists like Uncle Andrew is always betrayed by the greedy appetite that is the true master of the wicked.

Uncle Andrew's speeches reveal the heart of a magician. Digory reveals the heart of an adventurer in deeds, not speeches. He answers his uncle's high-flown rhetoric with common decency, common sense, and a simple, wholly conventional virtue. More than that, he answers Andrew's empty talk with action—a willingness to put himself at risk in the pursuit of what he knows to be right. "I'm sick of this jaw," he tells his uncle. "What have I got to do?" Digory willingly embarks on the adventure that Polly embarks on accidentally, and that Uncle Andrew would never dream of embarking on.

It should be noted, however, that it is virtue, not adventurousness, that motivates Digory to leave this world and follow after Polly. He takes the yellow ring because it is the right thing to do—the *only* thing to do, according to the code of honor to which he subscribes.

It is the spirit of adventure that makes it possible for Digory to overcome the fears that might cause him to shrink back from a life of vigorous virtue. Even in its hardships, the willingness to plunge into the unknown carries its own rewards. But pure adventurousness, ungoverned by virtue or any other larger purpose, can quickly devolve into thrill-seeking or a dangerous curiosity. As Paul F. Ford points out, Lewis viewed curiosity as more than a desire for knowledge. Curiosity is an *excessive* desire for knowledge, a variety of the sin of intemperance, according to the medieval tradition. And, as Digory and Polly find out in the ruined city of Charn, it can be exceedingly destructive.

It's not obvious exactly when Digory's healthy sense of adventure becomes idle (or worse than idle) curiosity. Having made it to the Wood between the Worlds—having, in a sense, completed his mission—Digory feels the urge to explore other worlds at the bottoms of other pools, in spite of Polly's doubts. When he and Polly find themselves in the postapocalyptic landscape of Charn, Polly is understandably eager to get back to the safety of the Wood between the Worlds. Digory makes a sensible argument, an adventurer's argument: "There's not much point in finding a magic ring that lets you into other worlds if you're afraid to look at them when you've got there."

By the time the children reach the bell and hammer in Jadis's hall of images, Digory's adventurousness has shaded over into morbid curiosity. The inscription on the pillar warns of danger, and Polly has the good sense to draw back. But Digory doesn't. He convinces himself that he'll go mad if he doesn't ring the bell. He claims to be enchanted already. His attempt to shift the blame for his actions is a bad sign. It is his own willfulness, not the spell of Jadis, that has him in its grip. Polly isn't buying his excuses.

Curiosity may be the characteristic sin of adventurers, but it's also a characteristic sin of magicians. And as Polly observes, Digory begins to look and talk and act a lot like his Uncle Andrew. "Why can't you keep to the point?" he asks. It's the same thing Uncle Andrew asked Digory when Digory proposed common sense against his single-minded willfulness. In an act of selfishness and meanness worthy of his Uncle Andrew, Digory physically imposes his will on the weaker Polly. It's a shocking moment—Digory's one truly dishonorable act—and it unleashes an avalanche of trouble that will echo throughout Narnian history.

✦

The postapocalyptic ruin of Charn is the magician's bargain carried to its terrible conclusion. Here is the desolation wrought by a woman who would prefer to be queen of nothing than not be queen. Jadis sold her soul for power, but it's a power she couldn't preserve. "Jadis, the last Queen, but the Queen of the World," she calls herself, and she seems proud of the title. She could hold her throne, however, only by speaking the Deplorable Word, the word that kills all living things but its speaker. By speaking the Deplorable Word she ensured that she would never again have subjects. But neither would she ever be a subject herself.

Digory asks the obvious question: what about the people who died when she spoke the Deplorable Word? The queen might be Uncle Andrew speaking of his guinea pigs: "They were all *my* people. What else were they there for but to do my will?" She goes on to explain what a common boy like Digory couldn't possibly understand: what is wrong for others is not wrong for a great queen. "We must be freed from all rules," she says. "Ours is a high and lonely destiny." It's the same language Uncle Andrew used, and Jadis has that same greedy, hungry look on her face as Uncle Andrew had on his.

As much as it would offend Jadis to say it (and as much as it would flatter Andrew), she and Andrew are different only in degree. Uncle Andrew, thankfully, does not have so vast a scope in which to wreak havoc, nor so much power to wield. But it doesn't make him any less wicked.

The Wood between the Worlds effects a remarkable change in Jadis. Her strength and beauty, her imperious bearing, everything that marks her out as a great queen and enchantress, are all gone. She can hardly breathe, and Digory and Polly find that they are stronger than the great queen whose hands had gripped them like steel pincers in Charn. The terror of Charn is terrified by this peaceful and life-giving place. Jadis's whole power is the power to destroy. It's the only power evil has—corrupting, destroying, twisting, despoiling, killing that which was meant for good.

There's no death or destruction or turmoil in the Wood be-tween the Worlds. There is only growth, peace, a verdant life force. It is an ideal place for those who are perfectly free of ambition—Uncle Andrew's guinea pig, for instance—for there is only being, no doing, and certainly no undoing. It is a perfect torment for Jadis.

Earth is apparently a good climate for the ambitious, however, and when Jadis gets to Uncle Andrew's study, she recovers nicely. She looks "ten times more alive than most of the people one meets in London." And Andrew suddenly doesn't seem nearly so terrifying as he did the first time we met him. He suddenly seems very much like a man who has gotten in over his head. For all his self-congratulating talk about being a great scholar and thinker, he sees now that he never really understood what he was doing—never got below the surface of the body of knowledge he considered himself an expert on. Uncle Andrew had fancied himself a kindred spirit of the great magician Faustus; in fact, he has more in common with Faustus's servant, who read from his master's book of spells and terrified himself by conjuring up the devil. Uncle Andrew is not the tragic hero, but the comic relief. Jadis despises the shrimpish, terrified creature who bows and scrapes before her, but she cannot deny that he has the mark of a magician on him, and she decides she may have some use for him. She takes him for a servant.

There is in all evil a certain degree of absurdity. As

Lewis wrote in his *Preface to Paradise Lost*, "mere Christianity commits every Christian to believing that 'the Devil is (in the long run) an ass.' "[3] According to long tradition, the one thing the devil cannot stand is to be laughed at. Perhaps this is why every villain in the Chronicles of Narnia is shown at one point or another to be ridiculous. Uncle Andrew, who seems genuinely terrifying in his first appearance, is portrayed as a thoroughgoing fool for the remainder of the book.

Perhaps Uncle Andrew's character is best summed up in his self-flattering fantasy that Jadis may fall in love with him. He indulges his fantasy only in her absence, of course, for her presence is so overawing that even Uncle Andrew isn't fool enough to imagine himself a suitable match for her.

Jadis herself comes in for ridicule too. When she announces that she is the Empress Jadis, a few members of the crowd gathered at the lamppost set up a cheer for "the Hempress of Colney 'Atch." Jadis begins to blush and bows slightly in acknowledgment of their praise. The people she has come to rule seem to be showing at least a little of the respect they owe her. She has no way of knowing that Colney Hatch is an insane asylum. But she does know mockery when she hears it, and it enrages her. It seems she's unaccustomed to anyone taking her less seriously than she takes herself.

The lamppost scene introduces another character: Frank

the cabman. Amid the swirling, shouting chaos of the street, Frank is a voice of calm and good sense. He misunderstands the situation in many ways. His suggestion, for instance, that Jadis "go 'ome and 'ave a nice cup of tea and a lay-down quiet-like" isn't well received, but his intentions are good. He appears to be the only grown-up in the crowd whose actions are motivated by kindness. When the situation gets more dangerous, and most of the crowd is backing away and Uncle Andrew is talking rather than acting, Frank hangs in, trying to soothe his horse even as his horse and his horse's new rider threaten to knock him senseless.

✦

When Digory and Polly take Jadis (and Strawberry and Frank the cabman and Uncle Andrew) out of our world, it at first appears that they have ushered them into oblivion. "My doom has come upon me," says the witch in a most matter-of-fact tone. She is no coward. Uncle Andrew, on the other hand, is. He is reduced to a babbling, self-pitying child *en route* to Narnia. "Is it the end? I can't bear it. It's not fair." There in the blackness of Nothing, it is the cabby's voice, a "good, firm, hardy voice," that speaks comfort and good sense. Again Frank doesn't fully understand the situation (he thinks they've either fallen down a construction hole or died) but his response is still the right one. If they are alive, he's thankful nobody has any broken bones. If they're dead, he reminds his companions that it's not the worst thing that could happen, and that "there ain't nothing to be afraid of if a chap's led a decent life." In either case, he feels, the best thing to do would be to sing a hymn. It's a simple act of faith and devotion; in such an uncertain situation, no other response could be so appropriate.

Lewis, by the way, did not enjoy hymns himself. He called them "fifth-rate poems set to sixth-rate music." But he didn't mistake his aesthetic judgments for spiritual insights. He held in awe those more sanctified (if less culturally polished) believers who did derive from hymns the spiritual edification that escaped him. "I realized that the hymns . . . were, nevertheless, being sung with devotion and benefit by an old saint in elastic-side boots in the opposite pew, and then you realize that you aren't fit to clean those boots."[4] Frank, it seems, is one of those uneducated working-class saints whom Lewis admired so deeply.

Frank's hymn gives way to another song. Aslan's creation song is life put to music. It comes from all directions at once. It sounds like the singing of the earth itself, and to Digory it is the most beautiful sound he has ever heard— "so beautiful he could hardly bear it." The old cab-horse is as affected by the music as anyone in the group.

The sky fills with stars, and the stars join the song. "Glory be," says Frank. "I'd ha' been a better man all my life if I'd known there were things like this." The cabman immediately understands the significance of what he's seeing. The Maker has a claim on him—his whole self, body and soul. "The heavens declare His righteousness, / For God Himself is judge" (Ps. 50:6). For Frank and the children, that's good news. The pure in heart rejoice in the scene. But for Uncle Andrew, who has committed so many crimes against creation, the voice of the Creator is a terror. "If he could have got away from it by creeping into a rat's hole, he would have done so."

The witch's aversion to the creation song is even stronger. She is a destroyer, the speaker of the Deplorable Word, an even greater enemy of creation than Uncle Andrew. She knows that this world is filled with a creative magic that is stronger than her power to destroy. The creation song that so gladdens the children, the cabman, and even the horse fills her with the hatred of impotence. "She would have smashed that whole world, or all worlds, to pieces, if it would only stop the singing." But she cannot overpower the magic that gives life to this new world.

When Aslan appears on the scene, the new-formed land explodes with heather and trees and rippling grasses. It's a riot of vegetation, more than the children can take in. Uncle Andrew stands right in the middle of it, a world taking shape around him, and doesn't even notice. Now that his experiment has succeeded, he's anxious to get back to the safety of his attic room. Having failed in his efforts to cajole Digory into stealing home with him, he now busies himself trying to steal the ring from Digory.

The witch confronts him: would he sneak away and leave her stranded? "Most undoubtedly I would," he answers. "I should be perfectly within my rights. I have been most shamefully, most abominably treated." Uncle Andrew suffers what Lewis once called the "Satanic dilemma." Satan, of course, didn't start out in hell. He started out in heaven, where every happiness was available to him. He fell from that state because he would rather be in charge than be happy. "In the midst of a world of light and love, of song and feast and dance, he could find nothing to think of more interesting than his own prestige."[5] New life bursts forth like fireworks in every direction. A whole world appears out of sheer nothingness. And all Uncle Andrew can find to be interested in is his own safety, his rights, his status, his digestion. He is curling inward on himself even as a world of never before seen wonders opens itself around him.

"Oh, stow it, Guv'nor," says Frank, who always seems to know the right thing to say. "Watchin' and listenin's the thing at present; not talking." Now is the time for taking in, receiving, marveling.

✦

Uncle Andrew's encounter with the witch changes the reader's view of him forever. He doesn't look so formidable next to a real magician. Something similar happens when the witch encounters Aslan. When she flings the iron lamppost bar at the Lion's head, he doesn't so much as blink. He keeps coming, undisturbed. The witch seemed ten times more alive than anybody else in London; her magic destroyed all life in her own world. She has seemed invincible. But she hasn't the power to make Aslan do anything. She doesn't even have the power to make him acknowledge her existence. In an almost slapstick moment, the terror of Charn shrieks and runs away.

Uncle Andrew doesn't even succeed in running away from Aslan, who is a little frightening even to Frank and the children. Andrew trips and falls down in the mud. He will find himself flat on the ground for much of the remaining story; the more he tries to protect his dignity, the more ridiculous he becomes. He persists in trying to get Digory to take him home. But Digory is an adventurer. He wants to know what will happen next. "I thought you wanted to know about other worlds," Digory taunts him. "Don't you like it now you're here?"

But when the witch is gone and the Lion is away, Uncle Andrew begins to return to himself. He begins to wonder how he might exploit the natural resources of this place. "The commercial possibilities of this country are unbounded," he exults. Nature is not a source of wonder for Andrew, but only the raw materials for the exercise of his power. He can't even think of the Great Lion as anything except an obstacle to his plans. The first step is to have the Lion killed. It's nonsense, of course, to think such a thing—not only because Aslan cannot be killed, but also because apart from Aslan there is no world to exploit.

"The land of youth!" Uncle Andrew crows, and it reminds Digory of his own dearest hope—a cure for his dying mother. Is it possible they might find a cure in this land? But Uncle Andrew isn't interested in such things. He's talking about himself—it's his favorite subject—and has no time even to think about his dying sister. Uncle Andrew's rebuff sends Digory straight to the Lion himself. Digory will soon find out what a wise move that is.

When Aslan speaks at last, he gives dominion to the talking beasts. "Creatures, I give you yourselves." This is the freedom that Aslan delights to give his creatures. Self-possession is a key theme throughout the Chronicles. Characters are always losing themselves, forgetting who they really are, losing their autonomy—and often because they try too hard to assert themselves—their power, their rights, their agenda. It's what Uncle Andrew is doing.

"I give to you forever this land of Narnia," Aslan continues. "I give you the woods, the fruits, the rivers. I give you the stars and I give you myself." The talking beasts are made to be in a relationship with their Creator. They were also made to be the masters of Narnia, Aslan's vicegerents. "The Dumb Beasts whom I have not chosen are yours also." But the talking beasts are to be kind masters to their speechless cousins. They are not, in other words, to treat them the way Uncle Andrew treats his guinea pigs or the way Jadis treated her subjects in Charn. As the devil Screwtape tells his apprentice: "Even in the nursery a child can be taught to mean by 'my Teddy bear,' not the old imagined recipient of affection to whom it stands in a special relation . . . but 'the bear I can tear to pieces if I like.'"[6]

The irony is that any talking beast who does begin to treat his subordinate beasts that way will eventually cease to be a talking beast and become indistinguishable from the dumb beasts. Something of the sort is what happens to Uncle Andrew. He has committed many sins against the lower creatures. Here in Narnia he is placed in a position lower than the creatures around him, though he never understands what has happened. When the animals approach this strange being with a healthy curiosity (a quality that Uncle Andrew lacks, by the way) he has no idea what they are doing. He has no idea they can talk; he hears only what he expects to hear from them: barks, growls, and howls. He lives so fully within his mind's closed system that new and unexpected inputs just don't get through. He somehow manages to filter out the obvious fact that Aslan can sing and talk; he decides he must have imagined it. Laughing animals should be a delight to him—perhaps even the sort of delight that might draw him out of himself and into a life of joy and purpose (not to mention a life of kindness to animals). Instead he sees nothing but a pack of animals baring their teeth at him.

The animals don't understand Andrew's speech either, and that makes it harder for them to understand what he is. After he faints some are convinced that he isn't even an animal, but a tree. Animals don't roll over; they stand up. They all agree that Uncle Andrew isn't a talking animal. The donkey gets it just about right: "Perhaps it's an animal that can't talk but thinks it can."

✦

Narnia is a country for a man to be king. And Frank the cabman is the obvious choice. He hasn't had much "eddycation," but neither does he need any to carry out the role Aslan has set aside for him. He possesses a royalty that comes from the inside out, not from the trappings of kingship or the exercise of power. His simple morality and straightforward manner define the *ethos* of the country Aslan is establishing. He will "try to do the square thing by" the animals, treating them as free subjects, not slaves. He "never could abide such goings on" as favoritism or the mistreatment of animals. Frank's rule over Narnia is to be marked by servanthood rather than lordship. He will be "first in the charge and last in the retreat."

✦

It was Digory who first brought evil into Narnia. Aslan gives him the grace of allowing him to heal the harm he has done. Where Adam and Eve failed Earth, Digory has the opportunity to succeed for the sake of Narnia, by resisting the temptation to taste a forbidden fruit.

Digory's quest is to pluck an apple from which will grow a tree to protect Narnia from the witch for centuries to come. The golden gates of the wall surrounding the tree are inscribed with a warning: "Come in by the gold gates or not at all, / Take of my fruit for others or forbear, / For those who steal or those who climb my wall / Shall find their heart's desire and find despair."

Digory's task is simple enough. He walks through the open gates and plucks an apple. But he makes the mistake of looking at it and smelling it before putting it in his pocket. He is beset by a terrible hunger and thirst for the apple—a fleshly yearning for the apple. He resists that temptation; simple appetite isn't enough to make a well-trained boy steal or break his promise.

The greater temptation comes from the witch, who has

climbed over the wall. She has eaten an apple, and it has given her her heart's desire. "She looked stronger, prouder than ever, and even, in a way, triumphant." She has received immortality. But from the new pallor on her face, Digory can see that she has also received the despair warned of in the inscription.

The witch doesn't bother appealing to Digory's appetite. She works him on another level. The apple in his pocket, she tells him, is the apple of youth and life. And even if Digory doesn't care to be immortal himself, surely he wants to see his sick mother healed. The words hit Digory like a blow. The witch has hit on his deepest wish. Digory has to choose between obeying Aslan and seeing his own mother healed.

Obedience is "the mother and guardian of all virtues," according to Saint Augustine.[7] Digory stands firm in his obedience because he trusts that Aslan's purposes are right and good. The Lion's tears were bigger than Digory's own when he told him of his mother's illness. The witch attacks Aslan's goodness: how good can he be if he makes Digory so heartless as to deny his mother a cure? But he made a promise, Digory insists. He didn't know what he was promising, argues the witch, and besides, nobody in his world has to know about his promise. He can go back to his own world alone and leave Polly behind.

The meanness of the witch's suggestion—the dishonor of it—jars Digory back to himself. He has no reason to side with the witch against Aslan. He flies back to the Lion. He completes his mission, and Narnia thunders with Aslan's praise: "Well done."

Digory has used Aslan's good gifts in the right way, and they are able to do the good work for which they were made. The tree that grows from Digory's apple is hope and happiness for Narnia. The same fruit, taken in the wrong way by the witch, is despair and horror to her. A piano doesn't have "right" and "wrong" notes. It just has notes. And, as Lewis pointed out in *Mere Christianity*, "every single note is right at one time and wrong at another."[8]

The golden gates swing wide for Digory because he was the right person to enter at that time. The witch can climb the wall if she wants, but she can't expect to benefit from the fruit. "All get what they want," says Aslan. "They do not always like it." The wicked choose to steal that which would be freely given—to sneak over the wall (or try to batter it down) when the front gate is wide open.

＊

No theological treatise can do so much as *The Magician's Nephew* to make the reader feel the truth of the creation story. "In the beginning God created the heavens and the earth." You've heard it so many times you may have lost the ability to marvel at that most marvelous, and perhaps the most fundamental of Christian truths: the natural world is of supernatural origin. Out of nothingness God spoke, and a universe appeared. And it was good. That's an astonishing thing to think about.

To put it in Narnian terms, the created world is fraught with magic. Behind the most mundane of earthly beings, objects, and events is a meaning and a power no less awe-inspiring than the Word of God who spoke the whole thing into existence. Yes, this is a fallen world. Dangers and temptations lurk everywhere. And yet the created order is also the raw material for a life of virtue. A thoroughly redeemed view of things, according to Lewis, opens the self to receive such delights as the created world has to offer.

CHAPTER SEVEN

Further Up and Further In
The Last Battle

 We have seen sadness in Narnia before. Under the rule of the White Witch, Narnians endured a hundred years of winter with no Christmas. Under the Telmarines, the animals and trees were silenced and Cair Paravel lay in ruins while murderers and schemers held sway. But the sadness that grows in the last days of Narnia, the days chronicled in *The Last Battle*, is another thing altogether. A despair approaching nihilism descends on the once-happy land of Narnia. Aslan, it appears, isn't who the Narnians thought he was; it's as if the world's moorings have come loose and everything is drifting toward emptiness. There is a sense of doom, of inevitable horror as the story progresses. Every hope is dashed. Every word of truth is neutered by a lie; every act of virtue is stripped of its power to make a difference.

Then, when it seems that things cannot get any worse, a new vision of the universe breaks like dawn. The vast drama of history turns out to be a comedy after all—a divine comedy. The sorrows and confusions and distortions of a broken and disordered world—the hardships that seem too much to bear—resolve into love and beauty and order and justice. Divine love overwhelms all. And your fondest hopes turn out to be only faint shadows of the solid pleasures that await the faithful. Your wildest dreams aren't wild enough—not nearly as extravagant as the joys God offers his people.

·✦·

When we first see King Tirian of Narnia, he can hardly keep still for joy at the news he has heard: Aslan has come back to Narnia. It is "almost too beautiful to believe." Roonwit warns that it's all a lie, but Tirian refuses to believe the wise centaur. A man of honor and piety, Tirian cannot imagine anyone perpetuating such blasphemy as counterfeiting Aslan's approach. It must be true, he insists. There are deceivers afoot in Narnia who have learned to exploit that kind of piety for wholly impious purposes.

Tirian's joy at Aslan's coming will soon turn to sorrow. For if indeed Aslan has come to Narnia, he is not the Aslan that Tirian thought he knew. The talking trees of Lantern Waste are being hewn down and sold to the Calormenes, supposedly at the command of Aslan. Talking beasts have been enslaved and worked by cruel Calormene taskmasters, again supposedly at the command of the Great Lion. It is utterly unlike anything Aslan has ever commanded before.

Jewel tries to make sense of it: perhaps the dryads have done something wrong and are being punished. But why would Aslan be selling logs to the Calormenes? Jewel is stumped. "He's not a *tame* lion," he suggests. His ways are not our ways. Jewel's feeble efforts to justify Aslan's ways arise from a pious impulse. The servant of Aslan wants Aslan to be justified. But he cannot convince even himself. For though Aslan has never been tame, he has always been consistent with his own nature. Talking trees have fallen before, and talking beasts have been enslaved, but always against Aslan's wishes, not according to them. If Aslan does not love his creatures any better than that, he is not Aslan. And neither Tirian nor Jewel can bear to think of living in a world without Aslan. "The worst thing in the world has come upon us," mourns Jewel.

In his rage at the Calormene taskmasters, Tirian commits murder. Even so, he submits to Aslan's authority. He asks the Calormenes to bring him before the Great Lion for judgment. He doesn't care if Aslan dooms him to death. Better to be dead than to fear that everything he has ever believed in and longed for is a lie. "It is as if the sun rose one day and were a black sun," Tirian says.

Tirian and Jewel are brought to the stable where Aslan supposedly dwells, and there they find that Shift the ape has set himself up as a grotesque priest, controlling access to Aslan and speaking on his behalf. The talking beasts are gathered around the stable in a sort of anti-tableau of the creation scene from *The Magician's Nephew*. There at the beginning of Narnian history the animals gathered joyfully around their great lord who, having already touched each of them nose to nose, gave them to themselves and gave himself to them. Here at the end of Narnian history, the animals gather in worry and bewilderment begging for a glimpse or a word from an Aslan who "can't be bothered talking to a bunch of stupid animals."

The words they do get come from the ape, who speaks only of punishment and slavery. "Times have changed," Shift says. "Aslan says he's been far too soft on you before, do you see?" Aslan, it seems, has cut a deal with the Calormenes to sell his people into slavery.

Shift's doublespeak sounds like something out of Orwell: "You think freedom means doing what you want. Well, you're wrong. That isn't true freedom. True freedom means doing what I tell you." The innocence of a little lamb cuts through Shift's shifting logic. The Narnians belong to

Aslan. The Calormenes belong to the bloody vulture god Tash. How could Aslan and Tash be friends?

Aslan and Tash are friends, Shift explains, because they're the same thing. "Tash is only another name for Aslan," he says. "All that old idea of us being right and the Calormenes wrong is just silly. We know better now." The gathered animals don't challenge the ape's claim but take it at face value. It makes them miserable—except for Ginger the cat, who doesn't believe in Aslan or Tash and sees an opportunity to profit from the credulity of his fellow Narnians.

Tirian cannot stand by and watch his subjects be abused and deceived. He knows full well that Tash and Aslan are not the same thing. Tash feeds on the blood of his people. Aslan shed his blood so that his people would be saved. But he doesn't get the chance to make his case. It's one of many near-misses in this story, moments that promise to be a turning point but turn out not to be. The disintegration of everything Narnians hold dear feels inevitable.

By exploiting the Narnians' most pious impulses, the deceptions of Shift and the Calormenes result in a kind of upside-down morality for the Narnians. Motivated by a desire to please their master Aslan, the Narnians do that which doesn't please Aslan at all. The raft-rat rides down the river on the carcasses of Aslan's holy trees calling to the king with no apparent shame, "Aslan's orders, Sire!" Horses submit themselves to slavery in the woodlots in the conviction that they are doing Aslan's will. Animals who would normally have fought to the death for King Tirian don't defend him from the Calormenes; they know that Aslan's authority is higher than the king's, and they believe Aslan to be on the Calormenes' side.

Even an act of common decency—the animals' ministrations to the bound Tirian—has its moral complexities. The animals know they shouldn't release a prisoner who is being held by Aslan's representatives. They can't resist easing his sufferings, however. But what if that turns out to be wrong too? "I don't care if it is," says one of the moles. "I'd do it again." The animals are convinced that Aslan has come back angry because of some unknown wrong they've committed. Not knowing what has made the Lion so angry is morally disorienting. The other animals are shocked by the mole's declaration that he'd give food and water to Tirian again, whether it's right or wrong, but in a world where people have begun to call evil "good" and good "evil," the mole has the right idea.

The Narnians' confusion arises from the fact that they put too much stock in what they can see. Shift has been able to deceive them because he has a visual aid. A donkey in an ill-fitting lion skin—in the dark—passes for proof with them. Tirian himself has a brief struggle when he sees the lion-donkey led out of the stable. Puzzle certainly isn't what Tirian expected Aslan to look like. But he has no way of knowing. He has never even seen a common lion, much less Aslan himself. "He couldn't be sure it was not the real Aslan."

That's not exactly a ringing endorsement of this Aslan's authenticity. But even so it's enough to start horrible thoughts in Tirian's mind. Then he remembers the absurdity of Shift's claims, and he knows this cannot be Aslan. His subjects have changed their understanding of Aslan based on what they have seen; Tirian measures the visual evidence in light of what he knows to be true, and the Aslan from the stable comes up lacking.

✦

There is an anti-Narnian hopelessness at about the first half of *The Last Battle*. Nothing helps. Jill and Eustace come when Tirian calls to them, but even help from another world won't be able to save Narnia. In *The Lion, the Witch and the Wardrobe*, *Prince Caspian*, and *The Silver Chair*, Friends of Narnia arrive to save the day. But there's no saving this day.

False hope—rising, then falling, then rising again—is what gives this story its rhythm. When Jill rescues Puzzle, it feels as if the deception is over and victory may be just around the corner. But it doesn't help. In the last days of Narnia, the deceivers always outmaneuver the champions of truth.

When Tirian, Eustace, and Jill free the dwarfs, it looks like the liberation of Narnia is beginning in earnest. "The light is dawning, the lie is broken," says Tirian as he attacks the Calormene guards, and it sounds very fine. Thirty dwarfs should be more than enough fighters to defeat the Calormenes at Stable Hill.

"Now, Dwarfs, you are free," Tirian exults when the fight is over. "Tomorrow I will lead you to free all Narnia. Three cheers for Aslan!" But there is no rousing cheer from the dwarfs, only sneers and sulks and growls. The old dwarfish cynicism overpowers whatever happiness they might have felt at being freed. Not only are they not thankful toward their liberators, they are downright suspicious of them, and especially of their talk about Aslan. "I've heard as much about Aslan as I want to for the rest of my life," says Griffle.

The dwarfs' shifty logic and willful misunderstanding is worthy of their ancestor Nikabrik. Tirian can't fool them with a donkey dressed up like a lion, they say. Tirian, of course, isn't trying to fool them into thinking Puzzle is a lion. He only wants the dwarfs to see how the ape had used Puzzle to imitate Aslan. "And you've got a better imitation, I suppose!" taunts Griffle. No, Tirian doesn't have any imitation, better or worse. He serves the real Aslan. The dwarfs insist that he show this real Aslan. They mock Tirian for having a fake Aslan to show, and they mock him for being unable to produce the real Aslan out of thin air.

Soon it becomes apparent what is really at stake for the dwarfs. As we already saw in *Prince Caspian*, dwarfs are political people first. Belief isn't very high on the list. What these dwarfs really want is political autonomy. "I don't think we want any more Kings," says Griffle. The dwarfs have no interest in helping Tirian regain control of Narnia. And if they're not feeling grateful for their rescue, it's because they see right through Tirian's motives—or so they think. Why would he rescue them if he didn't have some scheme for using them? The dwarfs are for the dwarfs. Off they go.

And so the disintegration continues. The ape's double-speak has already ruptured the connection between words and meaning. The dwarfs' behavior suggests a breakdown in cause and effect in human relations. Good deeds are met with hostility. The light of truth is met with willful blindness. Nothing in Tirian's experience has prepared him for the bad faith exhibited by the dwarfs. Their sufferings under oppressive falsehood didn't cause them to welcome the truth; it made them determined not to believe anything, true or false. Tirian has no way of knowing how many Narnians will feel the same way. There is very little left to count on.

Poggle's defection from the dwarfs to Tirian's party is a small source of hope. And when the party leaves to meet Roonwit and his band of fighters, the cheering spring weather seems an omen of good success. But it is just one more hope to be dashed. When Farsight the eagle finds them, he comes bearing bad news: Cair Paravel has been taken by the Calormenes, and Roonwit is dead. The centaur's last words offer very little hope for Narnia or for Tirian and his band: "Remember that all worlds draw to an end and that noble death is a treasure which no one is too poor to buy."

Tirian now realizes that Narnia is no more. But he is going to live as much like a Narnian as he can nevertheless. There is nothing left but to tend to his business: to "go back to Stable Hill, proclaim the truth, and take the adventure that Aslan sends us."

When they arrive at Stable Hill, however, they don't even get the opportunity to tell the truth—not the part about Puzzle and his lion skin, anyway. The ape announces that someone has committed the blasphemy of dressing an ass like a lion to deceive the beasts of Narnia. It will do no good now to show Puzzle; the ape has beaten them to the punch again with a lie that contains just enough truth to be very difficult to refute. Again it is apparent that no amount of good planning or bravery or quick thinking is going to save Narnia. All worlds draw to a close.

The faith of the Narnian beasts is quite moving in the final scenes on Stable Hill. After all the threats and abuse they've received from Shift on "Aslan's" behalf, they still long to see the Great Lion face-to-face. They are confused and deceived, but it seems they still don't quite believe that

Aslan is the monster that the ape has portrayed to them. When Shift offers the opportunity to go into the stable and speak with Aslan, (he calls him "Tashlan"), dozens try to take him up on it: "That's what we wanted! We can go in and see him face to face. And now he'll be kind and it will all be as it used to be."

When it comes down to it, however, the beasts are reluctant to step into the Calormenes' slaughterhouse, and rightly so. That's when Ginger the cat steps up to enter the stable. He has all the confidence and self-possession of a person who is in full control of his situation. But he doesn't stay long in the stable. He streaks out, terrified by what he sees—Aslan or Tash, or maybe both. He learns what is at stake in the blasphemous game he has been playing. Ginger, like Rishda Tarkaan, had believed there was no such thing as Tash or Aslan. He finds out to his dismay that he was wrong.

The Last Battle, when it begins, is a desperate affair. The true and faithful Narnians have little hope of victory. One of the saddest moments in all the Chronicles is the death of the bear in the first attack, "bewildered to the last." He dies muttering, "I—I don't—understand." Indeed it is all very hard to understand, and at this point it is hard for all but the most faithful not to wonder if the bear has died in vain.

The dwarfs, of course, are for the dwarfs, and they won't lend their considerable fighting force to either side. They choose instead to jeer from the sidelines. "In the last days mockers will come with their mocking" (2 Pet. 3:3). Lewis has come under considerable criticism for the dwarfs' use of the word "darkies" as they mock the Calormenes; it truly is jarring to twenty-first-century sensibilities. It is only fair to note, however, that to put the word in the mouths of thoroughgoing scoundrels is not to condone its use. As rotten as the dwarfs are, however, nothing really prepares the reader for their treachery and pure meanness in shooting the horses who come to join the battle. Their guilt is exacerbated by their jeering glee directed at Eustace after the crime: "That was a surprise for you, little boy, eh?"

The horses were Tirian's last hope, and that hope was small enough. When Calormene reinforcements arrive, all hope of winning the battle is gone. The Narnians' only hope now is that the Stable Door truly is the door to Aslan's Country.

✷

When the fighting reaches a crisis for Tirian and his band, things suddenly get better. Thrown into the darkness of the stable, they find that the darkness is a dazzling light. The first god Tirian sees in the stable is Tash. But Tash isn't waiting for the Narnians. He is there for Rishda Tarkaan. "Thou has called me into Narnia, Rishda Tarkaan," the great vulture-headed creature croaks. "Here am I. What has thou to say?" Speak of the devil, and the devil appears. As Lewis wrote in *Mere Christianity*, "If anybody really wants to know [the devil] better I would say to that person, 'Don't worry. If you really want to, you will. Whether you'll like it when you do is another question.' "[1]

The reader, perhaps, is as surprised as Rishda to see a false god appear in person. But even if Tash sets himself up as a rival of Aslan on the other side of the Stable Door, it is apparent on this side that he is at best "the Emperor's hangman," as Mr. Beaver called the White Witch. If the Calormenes choose to worship a devil, their souls will be handed over to him. Tash can take his "lawful prey" away. Tirian, however, is safe from him.

With Tash gone, Tirian is able to get a better look at the world behind the Stable Door. He is in the presence of the Seven Friends of Narnia, who appear as kings and queens in glittering clothes and fine mail. A few minutes earlier Jill's face had been covered in dirt and tears, and her clothes had been a mess. But now every tear has been wiped from her face, and she is robed in splendor. So is Tirian, he now realizes.

This is a place of wholeness and perfection. On earth, everything has a kind of perfection for every season: the glories of a tree when it blooms in the spring are different from the glories of a tree when it bears fruit in the autumn. But in this place, neither a tree nor anything else has to rely on time to reveal its glories. Here behind the Stable Door, the trees have the glories of the summer and the glories of the autumn together. And so it is that the Seven Friends of Narnia have all the beauties of youth and all the beauties of age—and none of the limitations of either—at the same time. Everyone is about the same age—or no age at all.

All physical infirmities are healed in this country. Peter's knee injury is healed when he is snatched here, and Digory and Polly stop feeling old. But make no mistake: they are not disembodied spirits. In fact, they have more physicality, more solidity here than they ever had on the other side of the Stable Door. As Lewis points out, it has always been the teaching of the church "that some kind of body is going to be given to us even in Heaven and is going to be an essential part of our happiness, our beauty, and our energy."[2]

In some Eastern religions, the soul's perfected state is the absence of desire. In the world behind the Stable Door, the perfection of soul and body both means the fulfillment of every desire. When Tirian sees the beauty of the fruit trees, he cannot help but doubt that such exquisite fruit could be meant for him. He doesn't know how good he's got it. As Peter says, "I've a feeling we've got to the country where everything is allowed." On earth desire is untrustworthy, susceptible to the frailties of fallen flesh; in heaven, desire is the surest guide to the good and right. In this place, everyone can do exactly as he or she pleases. And for the first time it will be fully, perfectly pleasing.

The dwarfs are there also. They, too, have found what they have been seeking, though it isn't what they need. "The Dwarfs are for the Dwarfs." There's a circularity about the statement, a closed-ness, that nicely summarizes the dwarfs' state. The dwarfian perspective is to have no perspective, to be impervious to outside input of any sort. Insisting on "seeing through" everything, they can't see anything. Refusing to submit to Aslan's authority, they have no means of submitting to his joys. They wanted autonomy, and that's what they receive.

The dwarfs are surrounded by the shining beauties of heaven, but they mistake them for the blackness of a dingy stable. "Are you blind?" asks Tirian. "Ain't we all blind in the dark?" Diggle shoots back. True enough. In their self-imposed darkness, the dwarfs are as blind as they can be. Lucy tries to help them understand. She can see fine, she explains. She can see that Diggle has a pipe in his mouth. But Diggle sees right through her. She obviously smelled his tobacco if she knows that. He mistakes the fragrant flowers of heaven for filthy stable litter. His spiritual discernment is no better. "Your wonderful Lion didn't come and help you, did he? Thought not," he sneers. Diggle is astonished that even now, in the face of defeat, in Aslan's obvious failure, Tirian and his companions are still playing at their wishful thinking.

Not even the presence of Aslan himself can make the dwarfs understand where they are. The Lion's growl, they are convinced, is a trick of Tirian's crowd. Somehow the dwarfs can believe that Tirian has brought a growling machine into the stable more easily than they can believe Aslan is there. "They won't take *us* in again," they boast. Aslan spreads a feast for them, but they mistake it for stable food—hay and turnip scraps and cabbage leaves washed down with trough water. "They have chosen cunning instead of belief," Aslan explains. "Their prison is only in their own minds, yet they are in that prison; and so afraid of being taken in that they cannot be taken out." The dwarfs cannot receive the grace that is extended to them. In the end, that's the only sin that can damn a person. The dwarfs carry hell inside them.

The dwarfs' self-judgment is a prelude to Aslan's great judgment in the next chapter. The talking beasts of Narnia stream past the Lion's judgment seat. And as each comes before the face of Aslan, his own reaction to his Maker determines Aslan's judgment. Those who look in Aslan's face with fear and hatred are sent away into the Lion's shadow. Those who look into Aslan's face with love are welcomed through the door. It's almost as if the beasts judge themselves rather than being judged. Which is not to say it is not genuine judgment. Elsewhere Lewis writes, "There are only two kinds of people in the end: those who say to God, 'Thy will be done,' and those to whom God says in the end, '*Thy* will be done.' All that are in Hell, choose it."[3] The beasts who walk into Aslan's shadow have made the same choice as the dwarfs in the stable.

The narrator is careful to point out that the legions of the saved include at least one of the dwarfs who had shot the horses. A perpetrator of one of the most heinous (certainly the most distasteful) crimes of *The Last Battle* is welcomed into the New Narnia. It is truly a marvel, and a testament to the breadth and depth of Aslan's grace. The question at the judgment seat isn't what you have or haven't done, but whether or not you will receive the grace that is extended to you.

Also among the saved is the bear who died in the last battle for Narnia; he still doesn't understand what has happened to him. But behind the Stable Door is a place for the healing of hurts; the reader's heartbreak at the bear's bewildered death is redeemed here, as he waddles over to the grove of fruit trees, "and there, no doubt, found something that he understood very much."

After the judgment, night falls on Narnia. Peter closes the door on the world that had brought so much joy—the world where the Friends of Narnia had first learned to know Aslan. And Lucy, though she knows she's in a better place, cannot help but mourn for the loss of the world that was dearer to her than her own. She knew her own world couldn't go on forever, but she had hoped that Narnia might. The reader can hardly help mourning along with her, for the reader has learned to love Narnia too. "It were no virtue, but a great discourtesy, if we did not mourn," says Tirian.

But Lucy cannot mourn for long. Aslan has called the Friends of Narnia to go further up and further in, deeper into the heart of things. As of yet, they are only in "the valley of the Shadow of Light," as Lewis calls the front porch of heaven in *The Great Divorce*.[4]

One surprise further up and further in is the presence of Emeth, a Calormene and faithful servant of Tash—at least he thought he was a servant of Tash. Aslan welcomes him: "Child, all the service thou hast done to Tash, I count as service done to me." Aslan's statement sounds suspiciously universalist at first—as if it were sincerity or faithfulness to one's own beliefs (whatever they may be) that really counts, as if, in the end, all religions point to the same thing. But Aslan clarifies: he and Tash are not the same, but utterly different—so different that Emeth's honest service couldn't possibly be mistaken for service to Tash. To put it another way, if Emeth had truly been seeking Tash, he would have found him long ago. "All find what they truly seek," says the Lion.

In an interview Lewis spoke of the person who desires God but hasn't found him yet: "I should say that this person has in fact found God, although it may not be fully recognized yet. We are not always aware of things at the time they happen. At any rate, what is more important is that God has found this person, and that is the main thing."[5] Aslan has found Emeth, and he receives the Lion's grace with all the wonder of the truly humble: "He called me Beloved, me who am but as a dog."

As Tirian and the Friends of Narnia go further up and further in to this strange and wonderful land, they find that things look more familiar, not less. It reminds them of a place they've been before. Slowly it dawns on them: they are in Narnia again. It's not the same Narnia they knew before, of course. That one has been put out like a candle. That wasn't the real Narnia anyway. It was only a copy. This is the real Narnia, and it has no beginning and no end.

Lucy has no need to mourn for Narnia, Digory reassures her. "All of the old Narnia that mattered, all the dear creatures, have been drawn into the real Narnia through the Door. And of course it is different; as different as a real thing is from a shadow or as waking life is from a dream." To put it in platonic terms, they left the cave and stepped out into the sunlight. The world of appearances has given way to the Real.

Heaven is not merely a state of mind. "Heaven is reality

itself. All that is truly real is Heavenly. For all that can be shaken will be shaken and only the unshakeable remains."[6] And reality is joy. It is the finding of the true self, like Shasta coming up out of Calormen to take his place as Prince Cor of Archenland, or Rilian coming up from oblivion in Underland to be Prince Rilian of Narnia again. At the founding of Narnia, Aslan told the talking beasts, "I give you yourselves." Here in the New Narnia, he gives them back to themselves, and true fullness of life begins. "I have come home at last!" rejoices the unicorn Jewel. "This is my real country! I belong here." What made the Old Narnia feel like home was the fact that it sometimes looked a little like the New Narnia, the true Narnia.

The New Narnians stretch the legs of their glorified bodies and run for sheer joy of the running. They are new creatures, body and soul—but not entirely new, either. The dogs are still dogs; they still have the desires and the excellencies that are peculiar to dogs. The eagle is still an eagle. And the humans are still human, now more than ever in their perfected states. Saying that "to err is human" misses the point altogether, even for humans who still live in the Shadowlands. Yes, all humans err, but that is not what defines them as human. All cars break down, but you could hardly say "to break down is automotive." A car is most truly a car when it cranks up and takes you where you need to be. Here in the New Narnia, the humans, like all the other beasts, have become what they were made to become—and free from error.

Deeper the travelers go into the heart of things, amazed that this place is meant for them. But they are welcomed all the way in, just as Reepicheep and Puddleglum and King Frank and all their dearest friends were welcomed before them. Then Lucy learns what we have suspected all along. This place is connected to our world too. The New Earth is just across the valley from the New Narnia, another spur off the same great mountain of Aslan. Further up and further in, all the real worlds join, the way spokes join at a hub. Aslan goes by a different name here on Earth. There at the hub, at the peak of the Great Mountains, perhaps the faithful will know all his names in all worlds.

The Friends of Narnia have come home at last, and for good. "The term is over: the holidays have begun. The dream is ended: this is the morning." The Chronicles are over for us, the readers. "But for them it was only the beginning of the real story."

.✳.

In the New Narnia, the sorrow and confusion of the last days of Old Narnia "fly forgotten as a dream." The crushing burden of helplessness and disintegration and seeming meaninglessness during the deceivers' reign now seems light as a feather compared to the solid joys of heaven. Death has been swallowed up by life. In heaven, "the good man's past begins to change so that his forgiven sins and remembered sorrows take on the quality of Heaven . . . the Blessed will say, 'We have never lived anywhere but Heaven.' "[7]

For now, though, we are living in the Shadowlands. From where we stand, the shadows on the cave wall look very real. But this world, like all worlds, will come to an end someday. We are always seeking our true country, and when we find something here that reminds us of it, this world can feel a lot like home. The fleeting joys of earth, however, are only homing signals; they aren't what we truly want. Their purpose is to point us in the right direction.

That's what the Chronicles do for us. They give us a taste of the joy that is sometimes painful, and they ask, "What do I remind you of?" They are a gleam of divinity on the human imagination, pointing us toward our true country, our truest selves, always calling us to go further up and further in to the life God offers.

BIBLIOGRAPHY

Andersen, Hans Christian. *Andersen's Fairy Tales*. Translated by Mrs. E. V. Lucas and Mrs. H. B. Paull. New York: Grosset and Dunlap, 1945, renewed 1973.

Ford, Paul F. *Companion to Narnia*. San Francisco: HarperSanFrancisco, 1994.

Hughes, Merritt Y., ed. *John Milton: Complete Poems and Major Prose*. New York: Macmillan, 1957.

Lewis, C. S. *The Abolition of Man*. New York: Macmillan, 1978.

_____. The Chronicles of Narnia. New York: HarperCollins, 2001.

_____. *C. S. Lewis Letters to Children*. New York: Macmillan, 1985.

_____. *The Four Loves*. New York: Harvest Books, 1971.

_____. *God in the Dock*. Grand Rapids: Eerdmans, 1994.

_____. *The Great Divorce*. New York: Macmillan, 1979.

_____. *Mere Christianity*. San Francisco: HarperSanFrancisco, 2001.

_____. *Miracles*. San Francisco: HarperSanFrancisco, 2001.

_____. *Of Other Worlds*. New York: Harcourt, Brace, and World, 1967.

_____. *Pilgrim's Regress*. Grand Rapids: Eerdmans, 1992.

_____. *A Preface to Paradise Lost*. London: Oxford University Press, 1941.

_____. *The Screwtape Letters*. New York: Macmillan, 1977.

_____. *Selected Literary Essays*. London: Cambridge University Press, 1969.

_____. *Surprised by Joy*. New York: Harvest Books, 1966.

_____. *They Asked for a Paper*. London: G. Bles, 1962.

_____. *The Weight of Glory*. San Francisco: HarperSanFrancisco, 2001.

Lindskoog, Kathryn Ann. *The Lion of Judah in Never-Never Land*. Grand Rapids: Eerdmans, 1973.

Macdonald, Michael H., and Andrew A. Tadie, eds. *The Riddle of Joy: G. K. Chesterton and C. S. Lewis*. Grand Rapids: Eerdmans, 1989.

NOTES

Introduction

1. C. S. Lewis, *C. S. Lewis Letters to Children* (New York: Macmillan, 1985), 53.

2. "Bluespells and Flalansferes: A Semantic Nightmare" in Walter Hooper, ed., *Selected Literary Essays* (London: Cambridge University Press, 1969), 265.

3. "Dogma and the Universe" in C. S. Lewis, *God in the Dock* (Grand Rapids: Eerdmans, 1994), 41.

Reality You Could Not Have Guessed

1. C. S. Lewis, *Mere Christianity* (San Francisco: HarperSanFrancisco, 2001), 41.

2. C. S. Lewis, *Miracles* (San Francisco: HarperSanFrancisco, 2001), 13.

3. Ibid., 14.

4. Lewis, *Mere Christianity*, 61.

5. Ibid., 42.

6. C. S. Lewis, *A Preface to Paradise Lost* (London: Oxford University Press, 1941), 97.

7. Lewis, *Miracles*, 206.

8. C. S. Lewis, *The Screwtape Letters* (New York: Macmillan, 1977), 42.

9. Ibid., 144.

10. Lewis, *Mere Christianity*, 30.

11. Lewis, *Miracles*, 208.

12. Lewis, *Mere Christianity*, 59.

13. "The Perfect Penitent" is the title of the chaper in *Mere Christianity* that deals with this dilemma.

14. *Mere Christianity*, 60.

15. I borrow this formulation from Thomas T. Howard's essay, "Looking Backward: C. S. Lewis's Literary Achievement at Forty Years' Perspective," in Michael H. Macdonald and Andrew A. Tadie, eds., *The Riddle of Joy: G. K. Chesterton and C. S. Lewis.* (Grand Rapids: Eerdmans, 1989), 96.

Myth Become Fact

1. Lewis, *Miracles*, 218.

2. "Myth Become Fact" in Lewis, *God in the Dock*, 66.

3. Ibid.

4. "On Three Ways of Writing for Children" in C. S. Lewis, *Of Other Worlds* (New York: Harcourt, Brace, and World, 1967), 29.

5. Lewis, *Mere Christianity*, 138.

6. C. S. Lewis, *Surprised by Joy* (New York: Harvest Books, 1966), 15–16.

7. Ibid., 14.

8. Lewis, *Mere Christianity*, 140.

9. Foreword to Kathryn Ann Lindskoog, *The Lion of Judah in Never-Never Land* (Grand Rapids: Eerdmans, 1973), 10.

10. Lewis, *Miracles*, 184.

11. Ibid., 218.

Finding Self, Forgetting Self

1. C. S. Lewis, *The Abolition of Man* (New York: Macmillan, 1978), 33–34.

2. Ibid., 35.

3. C. S. Lewis, *Pilgrim's Regress* (Grand Rapids: Eerdmans, 1992), 191–192.

4. C. S. Lewis, *The Four Loves* (New York: Harvest Books, 1971), 61.

5. The HarperCollins editions of the Chronicles return to the original British editions.

6. C. S. Lewis, *The Weight of Glory* (San Francisco: HarperSanFrancisco, 2001), 42.

7. Ibid., 37–38.

Remembering the Signs

1. Paul F. Ford makes this connection in his *Companion to Narnia* (San Francisco: HarperSanFrancisco, 1994), 337.

2. C. S. Lewis, *They Asked for a Paper* (London: G. Bles, 1962), 186.

3. This evidence may consist entirely of the authority of others whom we deem reliable. As Lewis points out, this counts as legitimate evidence too. Everything we know of history, for example, we know on the authority of people we deem reliable. None of us was eyewitness of the Napoleonic wars or the signing of the Declaration of Independence.

4. Lewis, *They Asked for a Paper,* 189.

5. Lewis, *Mere Christianity,* 28.

6. Lewis, *They Asked for a Paper,* 196.

Up from Slavery

1. Hans Christian Andersen, *Andersen's Fairy Tales* (New York: Grosset and Dunlap, 1973), 77.

2. Lewis, *The Screwtape Letters,* 37.

3. From "The Second Defense of the English People" in Merritt Y. Hughes, ed., *John Milton: Complete Poems and Major Prose* (New York: Macmillan, 1957), 830.

4. Lewis, *The Screwtape Letters,* 37–38.

5. Andersen, *Andersen's Fairy Tales,* 78.

Adventurer and Magician

1. Lewis, *The Abolition of Man,* 88.

2. Ibid., 83–84.

3. Lewis, *Preface*, 95.

4. Lewis, "Answers to Questions on Christianity" in *God in the Dock*, 62.

5. Lewis, *Preface*, 96.

6. Lewis, *The Screwtape Letters*, 98.

7. Lewis, *Preface*, 69.

8. Lewis, *Mere Christianity*, 11.

Further Up and Further In

1. Lewis, *Mere Christianity*, 46.

2. Ibid., 98.

3. C. S. Lewis, *The Great Divorce* (New York: Macmillan, 1979), 72.

4. Ibid., 67.

5. Lewis, *God in the Dock*, 62.

6. Lewis, *The Great Divorce*, 69.

7. Ibid., 68.